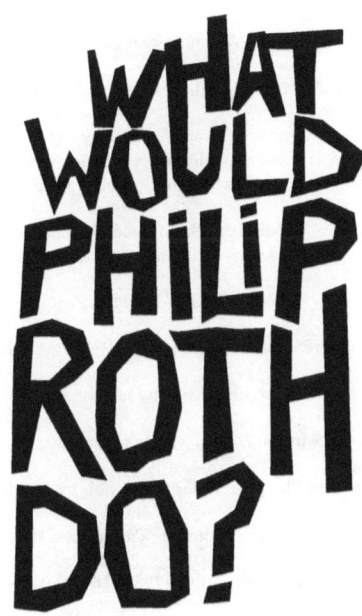

What Would Philip Roth Do? A Memoir

Published by Parentheses Press

Sheridan, Wyoming of registration

Copyright © 2025 by Matthew Check. All rights reserved

ISBN: 979-8-9916441-2-9

BIOGRAPHY & AUTOBIOGRAPHY / Memoirs

Cover and interior design by Jason Anscomb.

Names: Check, Matthew, author.

Title: What would Philip Roth do? / a memoir by Matthew Check.

Description: Sheridan, Wyoming : Parentheses Press, [2025]

Identifiers: ISBN: 9798991644129

Subjects: LCSH: Check, Matthew. | Banjoists --United States--Biography. | Jewish musicians --United States--Biography. | Bluegrass musicians--United States--Biography. | Bluegrass music--United States. | Jewish men--United States--Psychology. | Roth, Philip--Fiction. | Single people--United States--Psychology. | Unrequited love--United States. | LCGFT: Autobiographies. | BISAC: BIOGRAPHY & AUTOBIOGRAPHY / Memoirs.

Classification: LCC: ML418.C634 A2 2025 | DDC: 780.92--dc23

QUANTITY PURCHASES: Schools, companies, professional groups, clubs, and other organizations may qualify for special terms when ordering quantities of this title.

For information, email wendy@parenthesespress.com.

Printed in the United States of America.

PARENTHESES
PRESS

WHAT WOULD PHILIP ROTH DO?

A memoir by
MATTHEW CHECK

"NAZI TALK SMEGMA THE-CLAP- DIRTY WARTS?
HORSE DIRTY BOY?" JIMMY-DUGAN! TO ME UGH. AVOID-
DUNG TO ME THE-CLAP-
SMEGMA JIMMY-DUGAN!
BOY?" UGH,
WARTS? SMEGMA
UGH EBOLA
BABIES
AVOID- TOT
THE-
CLAP- SHABBAT
JIMMY
-DUGAN! TALK
DIRTY
WARTS? TO ME
UGH.
AVOID
SMEGMA "TALK DIRTY
SMEGMA TO ME" DIRTY?
SMEGMA REALLY?
JELLY- JELLY-
SOUNDING SOUNDING
PLOTZ? PLOTZ
"TALK DIRTY BABIES PLOTZ
TO ME" DIRTY?
REALLY? BIBLE+BAGELS CLASS
JELLY BOY? SMEGMA WARTS? EVERY THIRD THURSDAY
SOUNDING SMEGMA UGH. IN THE SARAH AND BERNARD
PLOTZ? SMEGMA AVOID LIVSCHITZ FAMILY LIBRARY
BIBLE + BAGELS CLASS "TALK DIRTY NAZI
EVERY THIRD THURSDAY TO ME" DIRTY? HORSE
IN THE SARAH AND BERNARD REALLY? DUNG
LIVSCHITZ FAMILY LIBRARY

To my father, Ron Check.
I'm sorry.

DISCLAIMER

Almost all the names in this book have been changed, except for those of my immediate family (much to their chagrin).

I've sometimes taken liberties with the order of events and recreated dialogue as best I could. My memory of events may not quite match that of others who were there. Life is always subject to interpretation.

As for Philip Roth—no, I never met him, in case you were wondering. The closest I ever came was a missed opportunity to bid on his typewriter, which was up for auction at his estate sale the year he passed.

Of course, I wonder what he would think of my creation. He'd probably hate it.

THIS IS A "SURPRISE INSIDE" BOOK

Remember when cereal boxes came with a secret toy buried deep inside the box? At Parentheses Press, we wanted to create that same emotion when moving through a book. Dig deep inside the pages and get your free gift. Or just scan the QR code above. This link works too: www.parenthesespress.com/mattsurprisegifts

INTRODUCTION

When I first discovered the novels of Philip Roth, I felt a deep connection. It was as if this author understood me in a way that no one else could. It was the absurdity I related to.

There were the scenes in *Portnoy's Complaint* when Alex's mother threatens him with a knife to get him to eat or in *Zuckerman Unbound* when Nathan *shtups* his lover Caesara O'Shea at the Hotel Pierre, only to discover she is having an affair with Fidel Castro. Then I came across Peter Tarnopol, the main character in *My Life as a Man*. His high-strung girlfriend Maureen claims to be carrying his baby, but little does he know that she has faked the results of her pregnancy test by getting a urine sample from a pregnant mom pushing a stroller in Tompkins Square Park. Insanity had never made so much sense to me.

As strange as it sounds, at one point, it turned into a dialogue. The more I read of Roth's books, the more I longed to talk back to him. So at one point I did. The voice in my head that I had conjured up did not belong to the young strapping professor from the seventies with the strong-and-dark mane nor was it from the elderly man of letters who wrote *American Pastoral*. Instead, the figure I met was sort of like Obi-Wan Kenobi—if you could imagine a Jedi from Weequahic. He was older and wiser and just a little bit sarcastic.

Eventually, he became a constant presence, offering up his opinion on my life whenever it suited him.

He still appears in my thoughts at unexpected times and if I had one complaint, it's that he's never as nice to me as I would like. Today, he greets me this way:

"Hi, Matt. Haven't seen you since your Mexican-Jewish girlfriend dumped you. Are you still putting jalapeños on your challah?"

"The breakup with Carmen was mutual, Phil."

"At least your songs about her weren't as sappy as your classic repertoire."

"Come to think of it, I broke up with her," I lie. *"But let's talk about you."* I know exactly how to respond to his ribbing. *"How's the Viagra supply in heaven, Phil?"*

"You're assuming I'm in heaven."

"Good point."

By now, Philip Roth knows my story, save for a few details. At least he knows the part where I'm twenty-five years old, a young, innocent, Jewish man who moves to Manhattan to go to graduate school. I have big dreams. I want to be a Hebrew Bible teacher-slash-bluegrass musician who eventually settles down with the perfect woman.

"I never understood that whole relationship with Johanna. What did you ever see in her? Or that girl with the sewing machine, the one who

made owls. What was her name?"

"You're jumping ahead, Phil."

Phil often pops into my life without warning, so it's very likely that he will appear in these pages as well. After all, I am putting my thoughts down on paper and he is often part of those thoughts.

I just didn't have the heart to tell him no.

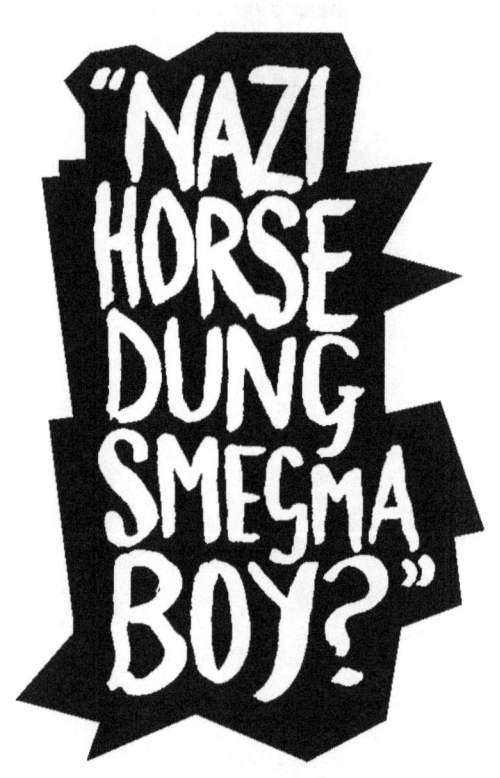

CHAPTER ONE

Bluegrass music and romantic conquest will always go hand in hand in my mind.

Perhaps that's because as I was graduating from high school and learning my first banjo rolls, I lost my virginity to a girl named Paulette Geller.

"Paulette Geller?"

"Yes, Phil."

"Could we get a bit of description? You know, writers do that with characters in their books."

"Tall, thin and blonde."

"Try harder."

"Knobby knees with a maturity beyond her years."

"Better."

I had always liked her. I always sat behind her in health class and stared at her hair, which smelled of strawberry shampoo. At the time we were learning the symptoms of things like herpes, syphilis and gonorrhea. My best friend Allen Grossman always referred to all of these diseases collectively as "Avoid-the-clap-Jimmy-Dugan," which came from the scene in *A League of Their Own* where Tom Hanks' character autographs this phrase on a child's baseball.

Our teacher was a crunchy heavyset lesbian who recommended that we masturbate as much as we wanted. I attended a liberal Quaker school in Philadelphia, so in addition to talking freely about whacking off, we even called our teachers by their first names.

One day during the sex unit, our teacher Marsha began by asking if any of us knew any sex positions. Hands were raised and she began to list our answers on the blackboard. I had seen sex scenes on Cinemax, HBO and the infamous hardcore channel 99 (probably the Spice channel), whose signal was often blocked but there were times when you could see a boob or a buttock. One time, as if a moment of heavenly glory had been shone upon me, the signal was totally clear for a full five seconds. There I saw a grown woman's actual vagina—bald as an eagle—with a penis buried to its hilt inside. There was moaning and the *pat pat pat* of pelvis to pelvis. In those five seconds I heard a phrase that I didn't fully understand because it was the first time I had seen pornography. "Oh yeah, milk my cock." *Milk my cock?* And from there the signal faded back into the mysterious ethereal ribbons of radio waves that masked the body parts.

So there was my heavy lesbian health teacher, listing the positions: doggy style, missionary, the scissors, the Japanese wheelbarrow. "Does anyone have any others?" she asked in utmost sincerity in her southern drawl.

Suddenly Allen blurted out, "You forgot the rim job!" The whole classroom burst into laughter. Xuan Lee, one of the Chinese exchange students, asked what that was.

Fruit-scented Paulette Geller raised her hand and was called on. "It's when you lick somebody's asshole."

The class fell silent. I was amazed. Had the girl of my dreams lathered somebody's grundle with her actual tongue? And if so, had she been propositioned or had she come up with the idea all on her own? I was fascinated.

Paulette was also the subject of my final semester photography project. I had mustered up the courage to ask her and she accepted—like it was a date. I photographed her with my Yashica medium format camera in black and white. My interest in her was piqued even more as I developed the pictures in the dark room. After the chemicals did their job in the floating basins, it was as if I triumphantly hung up an image of some mysterious Venetian smiling magically as she emerged in sepia and chrome.

After finishing up a second photo session, we sat together on the school lawn. It was a warm spring day. Having spent some time with her now, we talked about the end of high school and about college. She was going to Colby College in Maine and I was going to the University of Pittsburgh.

"I want to be an English major." Her voice had the faintest twinge of something between a whine and a purr. And she loved to draw out and pronounce her Ss like the girls on campus did that year as if it were some strange local feminine vernacular. "I just love the classicsssss." Her voice wasn't quite brusque, but not gentle either. If anything, I was drawn to the mysteriousness I felt in it. "And where are you going?" She hugged her knees close to her chest.

"Pitt. I'm going to be a biology major. Maybe I'll go to med school. Gotta make the parents happy."

"Indeed. So I'm leaving for Nantucket a few days after graduation to spend the summer there."

She was going to be taken from me just like that. I realized that I didn't want to lose her. I said the first thing that came to mind. "Can I kiss you?"

She laughed and looked at me, not saying anything. I remember wondering if she was thinking about rim jobs. But as she was lost in her silence, somehow I found the courage to lean in and kiss her. And when that happened, there were only two things in the universe that existed in that moment. The first was an immediate need to remain eternally attached to her lips. The second was the intense and rapid unexpected rippling beat of my heart, as if it were the steady attack of a banjo solo. In fact, the moment that I kissed her, it was just like the first moment that I had heard the banjo, for it felt like we had been separated from each other and had always meant to be reunited.

Bluegrass had come into my life earlier that year. At an open mic coffee house, one night I played guitar accompanied by my brother Jon on bass, the two of us banging out the notes to the Crosby, Stills and Nash song "Wooden Ships." We were the opening act for a band that had been invited to play as a guest artist: The New Hope Mountain Boys.

I'll never forget when the band was introduced. They were a group of four thin, stoic and hipster-looking guys all donning a combination of flannels and suspenders on a banjo, a mandolin, a guitar, a fiddle and an upright bass. The guitarist's face was thin and chiseled like a statue. When he introduced the first song, the cadence of his voice was as American as his name—Jim Finn—like he was a distant relative of Huck who had been written out of history.

Jim pointed to the banjo to count off and then burst into the opening chords of the song on his guitar. It was very simple—from A to G, back to A, up to E and back to A. A three-chord song and it was riveting. He began a song called "Little Maggie." From there, Jim commenced into a guitar solo that was clean, crisp and lightning fast. He weaved in and out of it, playing the melody he had just sung. It wasn't exactly formless, but it wasn't pretentiously formed and mapped out either. There was a certain modesty that the whole thing exuded. I recognized all of the scale patterns and the melodic phrasings that he was playing. Where was the amplifier? Where was the distortion or the wah-wah pedal that I loved to use on my solos? It was just a guy with his guitar. I wanted to know how to do this. He finished his solo and the group entered the second verse.

It was now the banjo's turn. I thought it lacked the decadence of an electric guitar, but it was just as powerful if not more so. Just like the way Jim handled the guitar, the banjo player picked with modesty and austerity. The fingers of his left hand leaped up and down the neck, while his right hand remained stationary by the bridge of the circular and metallic base. It was like seeing a beautiful woman without makeup. It was the truthful battle cry of this femme fatale Maggie—the protagonist of this seemingly mythical ballad—whoever, wherever and whenever she had lived.

I was punctured and pummeled by the ripple and roll of notes coming from the banjo. They pounced upon me as if suddenly I was Jacob wrestling the angel at the river at P'nei-El until dawn when I was finally felled by a sustained shellacking. A banjo solo is often described as an attack. And that is just what it felt like.

Being with Paulette wasn't unlike the act of playing the banjo. The night before she would leave for Nantucket, we unclothed in the candlelight of her bedroom. We touched, kissed, tussled and laughed. My fingers tiptoed up the inner thigh of her right leg, while my left hand was underneath her neck. Her reaction was one of quiet contemplation that ended in a long, eye-closed sigh. She was wet on all my fingers. She had always smelled good. Now there was a new scent that I had never noticed before: the unmistakable musky aroma of desire that was strangely arousing. This made me feel good about myself—she was ready, and all because of me. Van Morrison's album *Moondance* was playing in the background. I don't remember being nervous. I was excited. I was going to fuck for the first time! I climbed on top.

The only time that I had worn a condom was the night before—just to practice. It was the strangest feeling, like wearing a strange plastic sock. But this was the real thing. It was the first time I was entering anyone and it was the sensation of sheathing myself in something warm and moist, alive and pulsing that held me suspended in space. It was the greatest feeling ever. I was aware of some sound I had never heard before as I dug deeper, like a plowman in some field of Pablo Neruda poetry. Instantly she made the noise that they made on Cinemax and Channel 99—*ngggn*. I looked her in the eyes, kissed her and began to rock back and forth, in and out and side to side.

We rolled over and she got on top. I looked at the base of my upper body where she was attached to me as if we were a mythological monster, a combination of two distinct beings. She leaned forward to put her hands on my chest for support as she bobbed up and down like on a pogo stick and then back and forth like a jet ski. With her eyes closed she continued to make the sound: *ngggn, ngggn, ngggn*. Down below, the scent of desire was mixed with junky and jelly-sounding plotz. As I realized that this was what sex felt, sounded and smelled like, the thought dawned on me that I wasn't watching a movie. I was actually fucking and she was enjoying it too!

"Jelly-sounding plotz? Are you sure that's what you want to go into your book, Matt?"

"Yes, Phil. That is what it felt like."

"Yeah, why worry about details like that? I'm sure your editor will delete stuff like that in the final draft."

"Can we get back to my story, Phil?"

"Mum's the word."

"Make me cum," Paulette whispered in my ear.

"How?" I asked innocently as she continued to ride me.

"Talk dirty to me," *Dirty? Really?* I said the first thing that came to mind: "Milk my cock, baby."

We rolled back over and as I was on top, I looked into her eyes and I was close to finishing. I let myself enjoy it slowly as I kissed her. The sensation was somewhere between being emptied and a deep bellowing sigh, first slowly and then all of a sudden in rhythmic hiccups of spurting. After the contractions had subsided we continued to embrace. I could hear the crickets outside.

"What does that even mean?" she asked.

"What?"

"Milk my cock?"

"I heard it on The Spice Channel?" I almost heard myself ask.

"You watch porn?"

"Yeah, I guess so." I didn't mention that I watched it only when the TV station's blocking technology went down.

Then I pulled myself from her and I took off the condom. We lay there in a silent embrace for a while. But she had to get up early in the morning. I said goodbye to her, not knowing when I would see her again. I drove home that night feeling triumphant. But something happened as I slept. In the morning the satisfaction of everything that had happened had dried up. I imagined Paulette driving north on I-95 with the wind in her bangs, wearing a tank top, singing the lyrics to the song "Crazy Love," the second track on *Moondance*, the album I now eternally associate with the phrase, "Milk my cock, baby."

Two weeks later I got news that Paulette had been at a party on the 4th of July having fun. My longing changed to a combination of bitterness and resentment that I had never known before. I imagined her being entered through all possible orifices by prep school WASPy blonds with collared shirts and pink shorts.

It would be years before I would have the language to talk about it, though through this early romance, I already sensed that there was a part of me that clung to certain types—the type that creates a void inside of you that you never realized even existed. But once the crevice is opened, it's tough to ignore. I may never understand what inspires such emotions in me. Perhaps the mystery was in the fact that this girl seemed interested initially, and yet simply disappeared as if I had never existed. Over the summer, the scenario haunted me, made me bitter and yet, made me miss her even more. She was like a pet ferret that had gone missing in the woods. And no matter how much I searched, she would not resurface.

In desperation and longing, I turned to the banjo. Its twang might as well have been the cadence and rhythm of Paulette's voice drawing out her Ss over and over again. My right hand administered the thumb-in-thumb-out pattern, while the fingers of my left hand descended from the fifth, to the fourth, to the second fret. A melody emerged that I had never heard before. Like the first time I had heard the banjo, like the first time I kissed Paulette, this melody was like a piece of me that had been separated at birth and now we had been reunited.

It was an amalgamation of bluegrass and all the other musical influences that were important to me up until that point: the chord progressions of Bob Dylan, The Band, The Grateful Dead and the harmonies of Crosby, Stills and Nash and The Eagles.

While there was a familiarity to the song, at the same time there was something about it that was authentically me. I played it for Jon later and he was stunned by the lyrics in the chorus and the chords that accompanied the words: "I'll be here in the city / where the lights are bright at night / down inside I'm all alone / I should find a telephone and call you / so you can make me feel alright." I had produced a real song overnight. I called it "Drops of Rain." It was a colossal moment for me because I realized that the way Paulette made me feel had inspired me to write music on the banjo. It was clearly my outlet for unrequited love.

CHAPTER
TWO

When they are done fine-tuning the mapping of the human ge-
nome, I hope they take the time to look into the banjo gene—
there has to be one. Who would take the time to play something
over and over and over again that makes no sense initially and
that sounds awful? When I first discovered the instrument, for
some reason, I kept at it. And I don't exactly know why either. I
just knew that I had to play the banjo. It's the definition of some
Kierkegaardian version of faith. I worked tirelessly, seeking out
the existence of some deity—the twang of the banjo—that was
supposed to be coming from my fingers, but which I had to admit
to myself might not actually ever be manifested, even though I
hoped it would.

There was an exhausting despair in playing the banjo in the
beginning when my rolls would descend into failure (like a child

attempting to ride their bike without training wheels who crashes into some bush only to create scrapes and abrasions). And yet, I kept dusting myself off and getting back to work because there were also moments (and in the beginning it really was momentary) when the index finger followed the thumb, which followed the middle finger, and vice versa, and forward and backward and in and out, and it would miraculously form into something rhythmic and sequential that was for me nothing short of spotting a unicorn.

There is a rabbinic parable that rang true for me in moments like those. At birth our souls are split in two and our life's mission is to always find our other half: the *bashert*. In the moments that I was able to play the roll patterns, I felt as if I had been cosmically reunited with something that I had been separated from at birth, and now that I had found it, I was never going to let it go.

"You can't be serious? You're really going to just keep playing that thing? It sounds like shit," Jon said, coming into my room one night.

"What? It's so cool, check it out!" And then I began to play a cacophonous rendering of a basic roll pattern. "Quick, get your guitar and just play the G chord. It's fun!"

Jon was horrified. Someone had kidnapped his brother and replaced him with some strange stunt double. "Fuck you." He walked out, slamming the door. "And your banjo too, cockfuck!"

"What about your parents, Matt? What did they think about you playing the banjo all the time?"

"Well, Phil, my father just thought I was whacking off."

"You're gonna go blind!"

"I'm practicing."

"Yeah, right. You're thinkin' about Nancy Rotten-crotch and

Suzy Sweat-legs."

One night when I was ensconced in the middle of a banjo roll, he burst into the room wailing like a siren with a letter opener in his hands. "Prepare to die, banjo boy!"

My father played this game with me in my childhood where he would pretend to kill me with a knife. "I've got a knife," he called it. No one remembers the exact origin of this affectionate game, though I'm almost certain it all started one night after we watched *The Princess Bride* as a family and were all amazed by the sword-fighting scene where Mandy Patinkin proclaims, "My name is Inigo Montoya. You killed my father. Prepare to die!" From then on when Dad would tuck me into bed to go to sleep at night, he would hold his fist as if it contained a dagger and I would have to grab and hold it back in a tussle. By high school it was common for him to use a letter opener, and because of it I often kept scissors next to my bed, just in case.

This time I was ready for him. I tossed the banjo to the side, just in time to grab his fist with my right hand, and with my left, I grabbed the scissors. "Your days are numbered, old man!"

With that he caught my fist with his right palm. "You little shit. Stop playing the banjo and come downstairs for dinner! Your mother's makin' cutlets!"

But I could not stop practicing. Neither my brother's commentary nor my father's knife-wielding tactics could deter me (I have no story about Mom during this period, though she was suspicious of my actions as well). I was like a penitent man in search of a holy chalice that was just beyond some narrow ladder bridge that looked down into an abyss. It would be my salvation in a cup, goddammit.

I didn't know it at the time, but the banjo was going to change me. It wasn't obvious yet that it was going to be my companion through the trials of early adulthood. But it was clear that it was the only thing that gave me a sense of purpose as I waited to leave for college, as I moved into the dorms, even as I started my first semester of classes.

My second year at the University of Pittsburgh I was studying English literature and Spanish when one day I got a call from "You forgot the rim job" Allen (my friend from health class who referred to all STDs collectively as "Avoid-the-clap-Jimmy-Dugan").

"Are we going to Madrid or what?"

I had never really been abroad except for Aruba on family vacations where we sat on the beach with fat Venezuelans wearing gold neck chains and brightly colored Speedos—and one volunteer trip that I took with my high school to go to Costa Rica when I was seventeen (also the time when I woke up in the jungle with a tick on my penis). But besides that, I hadn't been out of the United States of America and so I had been apprehensive and putting it off.

"I'm not sure," I said, gritting my teeth.

"Come on, dude!" Allen sounded irritated. "Get your shit together already. It's gonna be awesome." Allen was at NYU and had been thinking about studying abroad for a while already. My application was due and he was calling to remind me.

I didn't want to tell him what I was really thinking. *Was it even safe to go to Spain since that was where the Inquisition happened? Sure, it was half a millennium ago, but maybe there were some residual effects.*

"Sure?" I heard myself asking hesitantly.

"Matt, it's gonna be awesome. We're gonna bang Spanish chicks. Get your application in."

As he said this, my *Norton Anthology of English Literature* was sitting there in front of me on my desk with a picture of Shakespeare in his iconic accordion-like turtleneck. It was as if he were staring at me and begging me not to leave him in Pittsburgh, while Allen was tugging at me to go with him to Spain on the other end of the telephone. It dawned on me that *schtupping* Spanish women would be much more interesting than reading about the English Renaissance in Pittsburgh (even if there were antisemites lurking in the shadows somewhere).

And that's how I brought the banjo to Spain at twenty years of age. We landed ourselves a beautiful apartment in a neighborhood called *Atocha*, with narrow streets made of cobblestone. It was like a European car commercial with classical music in the background, old women with cracked raisin skin waving *Buenos Dias* with their handkerchiefs at you from a little balcony. We shared a bedroom with two twin beds, a living room and a kitchenette. We even had a bidet in the bathroom (which I swear I never actually tried). It was a far cry from the dorm room back in Pittsburgh.

Our balcony overlooked the front of our street, *La Calle de San Blas*. That was where I practiced the banjo. It was so picturesque the first time that I sat down to play my rolls. I was like Noah seeing the rainbow as the floodwaters receded into dry land below.

The customary blessing that a Jew says when he or she does something for the very first time is the Shehecheyanu. Though it is traditionally recited at the beginning of multi-day festivities (the first night of Hanukkah or Passover)—it is also common practice for Jews to say the phrase *"Shehecheyanu V'kiyamanu"* when something personally significant happens to them.

So I whispered it to myself as I played my first rolls on the balcony of our new Spanish home. It was in a way a unique moment in my life. It was a time when I practiced like never before. I was mostly obsessed with the recordings from Old & In the Way, the bluegrass band from the early 1970s with Jerry Garcia (the lead guitarist from the Grateful Dead) on banjo. I studied the sound of his banjo solos for songs like "Pig in a Pen," "Midnight Moonlight," "Love oh Love Please Come Home" and "Until the End of the World Goes 'Round."

Allen had also brought his guitar. He embraced the banjo and humored me by learning the backup chords to all of these songs. There was nothing intentional or planned about the *bluegrassification* of our Spanish home. It happened organically. While most of Madrid was listening to Shakira's *Whenever* and the new Alejandro Sanz *Unplugged* album in the winter of 2002, we were like two *moranos* playing bluegrass in our apartment, as if we were the last two Jews hiding the precious and last Hanukkah menorah in Spain from Torquemada, while the rest of our people had been banished east to Constantinople.

We lived just steps from the famous Buen Retiro Park and near two of the iconic museums of the city: the Prado and the Reina Sofia. We were just a walk away from the greatest paintings in history by Velázquez, Rubens, Caravaggio, El Greco and Picasso. The *jóvenes* of Madrid walked around in loafers and button-down shirts that they tucked into their tight-fitting jeans. It was common to see lovers in the park kissing with passion while somehow smoking their own individual cigarettes seamlessly. All of these natural street scenes—any of which could have been the subject of a beautiful photograph for someone like Cartier-Bresson—all of it was suddenly disturbed by the jarring twang of bluegrass.

There I stood with my banjo, and Allen with his guitar, both of us wearing jeans and flannel shirts, busking for the newly printed currency that had come out for all of Western Europe that January, the euro (Spain had changed over from the peseta the week before we arrived). Our American-flannel-and-ripped-jean thing made us look like two hobos who had just gotten off a freight train. Spain was a far cry from any existence we had known.

One time an old man strolled by us in the middle of me soloing. He was wearing an ascot and was draped in a checkered blazer that hung around his shoulders as he probably considered some private *pensamiento* about the Franco era. And then he was wrested from his thoughts thanks to us.

"*Tócalo Mateo!*" Allen shouted, as I launched into the opening notes of my attack on "Little Maggie."

"Hmmf," the old man said in response. His distaste wasn't even a proper word. But it was easy to understand what he was feeling: *Who are these people? What are they wearing? What is this music? WHAT is that thing that he is playing? It's almost 2 p.m.—time for my siesta and then to cheat on my wife with my mistress.* He walked off into the distance.

When we weren't busy bringing bluegrass to Spain, or I wasn't practicing on our balcony, Allen and I would frequent the jazz café *Populart*. We watched live music amongst Spaniards who wore leather jackets, smoked cigarettes and had greased-back hair. They all looked sleek, mysterious and important. It was as if they were part of some secret club and I wanted in. As I sat there, I couldn't help but imagine all the guys with their five o'clock shadows as conquistadors just home from the new world, having shed their feudal armor, their steeds and their swords with which they had conquered and pillaged (much like how I have always imagined all Germans to have blond hair and blue eyes in SS uniforms, telling me to get off the train and just throw my luggage in the pile over there).

One night at *Populart*, I was by the bathroom on my cell phone telling Jon how things were going with my classes and life in Madrid, when a woman approached me. She began talking to me in Spanish as if I was a native and not even paying attention to the fact that I was in mid conversation with someone else on my cell phone.

I told Jon I had to go, because there was actually a real-life Spanish woman all of a sudden speaking to me (and all of her own volition too).

As I hung up the phone she said, "Nice to meet you," and continued without me even saying a word. "Where are you from? I love the music here. Do you like jazz too?" She was so person-able—and in another language too. She spoke to me quickly, in that low monotone Spanish vernacular with pursed castellano lips. She was beautiful with long hair, dark eyes and that classic Euro-pean angular face. I thought it strange that she was chatting me up. At first I wondered if there was someone behind me that she had mistaken me for, but I just went with it.

"*Soy Isabella.*" I was amused that she had the same name as the queen that expelled my people in 1492, the queen who also (according to lore) had the worst stench because she refused to bathe and so all of her subjects would avoid standing downwind. *La Reina de la Stank*, I thought privately.

I invited her and her sister Sofia to sit with me at the table with Allen. I attempted to impress upon them the basic Spanish phrases I had learned in class so far that semester, "Estoy muy excitado para vivir en España."

The two women I had just met began to cackle out loud uncontrollably.

Later I would learn that the word "excitado" in Spanish means sexually aroused. I'd told them that Spain really gave me a hard-on.

There were other Spanish textbook phrases I enjoyed practicing that night. "¿Tu eres estudiante?" "Me gustan tus pantalones." As we talked I couldn't help but imagine the ancestral version of these two beautifully thin Spanish women in little diadems and puffy dresses discovering two Jews in their midst.

That night, I spoke more Spanish than ever. When I used up all of the phrases that I had learned in class, it was as if I had played a five-hour-long gig and had no more licks to pull out of my pocket. So I did what any respectable man would do—I turned to alcohol. I ordered us more and more drinks as my Spanish became more and more fluid. I was drinking wine—Isabella liked whiskey. I tried to get to know my new *madrileña*, who I learned was working in an art gallery in La Puerta Del Sol, had a poodle and was as she put it, "*Pobre, pero feliz.*" She pronounced *feliz* with the Castillian "th" sound (*feleeth*). Who would have thought that even a lispy consonant would inspire? I suddenly wanted to possess my poor, but *feleeth* Queen Isabella—La Reina de la Stank (as long as she was downwind).

Later that night, Isabella was drunker than I was, could barely walk and fell into my arms in some side alley and we began to kiss in the rain. We had stumbled out into the streets together, long after Allen had escaped her sister who apparently was the drunkest of us all and who I would find out later happened to be an angry Marxist concerned about the capitalist corruption of George W. Bush who began calling Allen all sorts of things that end in the suffix ista: Racista, Fascista, Capitalista!"

By the time that Isabella and I entered my apartment, it was around 3 or 4 a.m. We were on the couch, where we continued to kiss in the dim light of the one living room lamp. I didn't want the buzz to wear off. We had an unopened bottle of Rioja in the kitchen. I uncorked it and poured us two glasses. I went to the CD player and without thinking, put on Old and In the Way. Jerry's banjo could be heard while we were on the couch. Her body was thin and birdlike as I undraped her tank top and then her bra. "*Ay, Mateo,*" she purred.

But then she slapped me in the face. Its sting caught me off guard. I didn't know why she hit me or what I was supposed to do in return.

I said the first thing that came to mind.

"What the fuck did you do that for?"

"You are a rapist," she told me in her drunken queenly vernacular of the Inquisition. "Americans only want one thing." I thought for a second that this meant that I had somehow been too forward, that things were finished and that she would be leaving. But instead she dug her nose into my ear and commanded me with a whisper, "Hit me, damn it."

I was confused. Was this some Inquisition-era ritual? A minute beforehand she had called me a rapist and slapped me. Now she wanted me to hit her? I was suddenly scared. It's true that I had been raised by a father who liked to role play killing me with a knife, but I had never known real violence. I had *never* hit anyone. Maybe I smacked my brother once but even if I did, it would have surely hurt my flimsy wrist. If anything I had definitely never *schtupped* someone that wanted to fight and fuck at the same time.

Yet for some reason I listened to her like an obedient student and gave her a light *potch* on the *tuchus*.

"Oh Mateo, again."

"Again?"

"Si, mi amor."

She apparently liked it. It was like I was in an Almodóvar film.

I spanked her again—hard.

"Ay!" she barked.

She grabbed my head with one hand and kissed me longingly as if it were in the final throes of her paramour being shipped off to sea. I had never seen a woman turned on like this before—she was like Sigourney Weaver's evil Zuul in *Ghostbusters* as she suddenly descended from my neck, to my clavicle, the base of my sternum, below the navel, kissing the bone of one hip and then the other as well—as if it were a ritual necessary for crossing the threshold into uncharted territory.

I felt my underpants yanked downwards and I was suddenly freed like a Jack-in-the-box. There was no hesitation on her part to play with me like I was one of the sculptures in her art gallery. I was a total stranger to her—my body, my odor. But she paid it no mind at all.

When she saw my penis, she suddenly stopped. There was a deadly silence (except for Jerry and his banjo solo coming from the CD player) as she gazed at my most intimate part, with an expression somewhere between confusion and intrigue—which is never a good sign for a man. Was it my size? Was there too much hair? Did Spanish guys shave themselves? Maybe she didn't like the way I smelled? I could wash myself if she wanted—I was secure enough to use the bidet if I had to. It would just take a second.

"Were you cut as a baby or something?"

"What?"

I then put two and two together and realized that she was talking about the fact that I was circumcised. *La Reina de la Stank* had never seen a nipped tip? It was her first time being with a Jew apparently.

"So much for being exitado, Mateo."

"Good one, Phil."

She must have been accustomed to foreskin and smegma (ugh, smegma). But before I could validate this, she quickly ascended back up my body in a flutter of kisses, placing her finger on my lips once she arrived at my face.

"Mateo, yo quiero hacerlo, pero estoy, como se dice en inglés, on the rag."

All I had to hear was the phrase, "on the rag." Who cared whether I was circumcised or whether my nether regions didn't smell pleasant? I wasn't having sex with a complete stranger while she was on her period. I was fine with cuddling and I was happy to make her a tortilla española in the morning. I could play her a little banjo too, but the sex could wait. Now was my chance to prove that I could be a man of chivalry—even if I was a Jew. So I told her how I felt.

"Not tonight."

She slapped me again. This time the slap was much harder than the first time. What was next? Was I going to be forcibly converted to Catholicism?

"What the fuck?" I yelled.

"¿Tú eres una mariposa?"

Now I was gay? I suddenly pictured the headlines in Madrid's

daily *El Pais* the next morning *"Gay Americano Judio muerto por no hacerlo con el rag."*

"Was the butchering of the Spanish language intentional here, Matt? In other words, was this something you were expecting your editor to fix?"

"No, Phil, I think it adds a little bit of color, don't you?"

"Gotcha."

As if the violence of the Inquisition and the trauma of my people's expulsion hadn't been enough? Now I would be publicly mocked in some plaza where they pronounce the z as a th. *"Si, El Judio está en la platha...th th th."*

I didn't even have time to respond to *La Reina de la Stank* calling me gay. She was suddenly gathering her things in a blind and drunken rage. She lit a cigarette and blew the smoke into the darkness.

"Don't call me, Mateo."

Well, at least that was a relief. She had given me a phone number so long that I wouldn't have begun to know how to dial it. Did I use the country code +34 if calling from an American cell phone in Spain? What about the code for Madrid?

She dressed and grabbed her things. I heard the rustle of her keys and the slamming of my front door. Two minutes later, the click-clack of her heels could be heard out on the street as she walked down San Blas. I went to the balcony and watched her walk away.

For some reason I longed for her instantly (even though she had apparently accused me of rape and then tried to rape me herself). The manner in which she had left me was a strange aphrodisiac, regardless of the reason.

"Isabella!" I shouted, sounding not unlike Stanley calling out for Blanche. "Isa-BELLLLLLLLL-A!"

"*¡Cojones!*" she spat on the street and stormed off while still smoking. I made a mental note to look up this word in my dictionary later. "*¡Eres una puta mierda!*"

It was as if I had dropped a delicate piece of china from my fingers and was watching it smash to thousands of shards on the floor with my head in my hands in utter disbelief. I realized in that moment that Paulette was the only one in my life that had inspired such emotion. Now I was feeling it again years later. I began to cry, snottily—like Ben Stiller at the end of *There's Something About Mary* when he said the line, "Brett Favre!"

But there was suddenly a melody that I was humming. And the strangest thing was not how quickly it came to me, but the fact that it was so familiar—as if it were already written and I had been waiting for some experience like this to come along so that the song could be manifested in reality.

The lyrics came to me almost effortlessly. "*Como si fuera la luz de la luna / te diera la risa de tus sueños.*" (As if the light of the moon could give a smile to your dreams.)

"*Hey, Matt, Phil here.*"

"*Yes, Phil?*"

"*Your editor is talking to me on the phone.*"

"*Really, Phil?*"

"*Yes, Matt. She wants to know if she should correct the Spanish grammar of your song lyrics.*"

"*There is nothing wrong with them.*"

"*Okay, if you say so. But just in case, here is her edit: Como si la luz de la luna pudiera dar una sonrisa a tus sueños.*"

Who knew what I really meant, or if it was even grammatically

correct? The fleeting nature of the moment made it so intense. Was it similar to the way that I felt about Paulette? Not really. But it still came from this place inside of me where both my love for the banjo and my desire to find love were obviously occupying the same real estate.

In the wee hours of that morning as I dozed off, I was reminded of something bigger than myself: the notion once again that romance and music were inextricably linked for me. It was like discovering some coveted superpower that few possessed. And it was the Paulettes and the Isabellas that brought it out in me, the women who left. For some reason, a fleeing woman was so much more attractive than someone who wanted to stay. Was romantic rejection apparently the ultimate aphrodisiac for me? Was that the recipe whose ingredients were just sitting on the countertop of experience, waiting for a chef-of-life to come along, apply them all to a bowl and stir them into the concoction that was my particular version of desire and its relationship to unrequited love?

In the morning when I came to, Allen was standing over me. Later I would play him the song and he would be impressed but at that particular moment, he just looked genuinely relieved that his roommate was okay.

"Did she hurt you? I heard lots of yelling and smacking."

"She tried to convert me."

CHAPTER
THREE

In my final months of college, I wrote an essay about the banjo as part of my application for a volunteer experience in Israel. Sure, I mentioned that my Jewish identity was important to me, but mostly I wrote about how I wanted to inspire people with bluegrass music.

"At least that's the cockamamie thing I was telling myself at the time."

"Why boychik? Because you were a spoiled kid from an upper-middle class family who had just majored in English literature, hadn't had any internships nor resume-building jobs to speak of, so you thought you'd kick the can down the road an extra year rather than sell paper for your father?"

"I knew there was a reason I picked you for my memoir, Phil."

"We're cut from the same schmatta, Matt. Don't forget it."

I was easily accepted to the program sponsored by the immigration service of Israel much to my parents' chagrin, who were afraid that I would move to the Holy Land permanently. (I had always done too much "Jewish shit" as my father once put it).

I arrived in Haifa on a hot August day in 2004 with just one backpack of clothes, my banjo and my enthusiasm for bluegrass music. I was proud and excited. It might as well have been just as I described it in the opening sentence of my essay: "In Israel I will build and be rebuilt through my banjo!"

My first assignment was working in an old age home in Kiryat Eliezer, serving meals and keeping the kitchen tidy. Each day music hour was held in the bomb shelter (which is less ominous than it sounds because there are bomb shelters in most buildings in Israel).

The director thought that playing for the residents might bring a bit of joy to their otherwise monotonous days. At his request, one day I walked to the front of the room holding my banjo. I stared out at a sea of wheelchairs, canes and oxygen tanks. These were Holocaust survivors and heroes from the Arab-Israeli wars.

"Shalom," I said, "This is my banjo! *Achshav, ani m'nagen b'shvilchem, ha'foggy Mountain Breakdown!*" (Now, I'm going to play you "Foggy Mountain Breakdown!")

I launched into the opening roll pattern of one of the most iconic songs in the bluegrass canon. This was why I had come to Israel, to change people's lives with songs like this one. The banjo meant so much to me. I knew it would help other people.

At first I wasn't sure whether I was making a difference for the elderly in the last years of their lives, with their sunken eyes and their number tattoos, but at least I was trying. These people had been through so much and I wanted to offer them a brief moment of joy. I gave it my all, banging out my banjo rolls as if I were on a stage in a packed auditorium.

Not even minutes later the room was nearly empty. One of the last to leave was a woman attempting to flee with her walker in terror. She didn't make it to the exit quickly but she did manage to get out.

None of them had ever heard bluegrass and they didn't know what to make of it. It occurred to me that perhaps the banjo's twang was worse than the Majdanek flashbacks of the walker lady's testimony against John Demjanjuk.

My next assignment was giving guitar lessons to Russian immigrants in a basement which also turned out to be a bomb shelter. I had been tasked with teaching them to play guitar, but I had nefarious plans. I figured that we could start with the guitar and then I'd subtly suggest a new option, asking coyly, "So, have you ever heard of the banjo?"

On my first day, only two people showed up. They were both skinny, blond-haired, blue-eyed teens with shaved heads, tight black jeans and Metallica and Megadeth t-shirts.

The first one sat down and explained why he was here. "Do you know any Def Leppard?"

The second one chimed in. "How about Kiss?"

They only wanted to play along to the tapes they had in their homes. It would have been a fascinating experiment to have played bluegrass music for these two kids (almost as fascinating as the amazing Hebrew they spoke with a Russian accent which was quite exotic to me). But I didn't even attempt this. Instead I showed them how to play power chords on guitar along to the closest song I really knew from childhood that was at least remotely related to death metal: Green Day's "Welcome to Paradise."

I was starting to come around to the fact that the banjo was not going to be part of the Zionist ethos as I had hoped. In fact, the only people that listened to my banjo in Israel were not Jews but Arabs.

In the neighborhood of Wadi Nisnas, I worked at a church, playing checkers and making art projects with a dozen kids in the game room, and sometimes playing soccer with them in the courtyard. They were Christian Arab-Israelis who were citizens of Israel (though they all had relatives in the West Bank and Gaza). The week before Christmas I brought my banjo with me. I had worked up a bluegrass version of "Jingle Bells" and had no idea at this point how it would be received.

"Dashing through the snow in a one-horse open sleigh." So far, so good. Everyone was singing along in English.

It was time for the chorus "Jingle bells, jingle bells…" However, I was the only one still singing in English. They knew the words to the song, but they were singing along in Arabic.

It was a surreal moment. I was accompanying a dozen Christian-Arab children singing Jingle Bells in Arabic while all wearing red Santa hats. They also called Santa Claus "Papa Noel."

Later that day we decorated a Christmas tree—the first of my life. It was not lost on me that in coming to the Holy Land I had failed at delivering the gospel of bluegrass to Israeli Jews and ironically had kind of returned it to Christianity in the land of its origin instead.

When I wasn't volunteering, I often used my free time to attend open mics. My favorite place was called Danny's Art Bar, located in a village just south of Haifa called Ein Hod. One Friday night there was a chalkboard outside the entrance with information about the guest artist in simple script: "Tonight: Maya, 20:00."

I walked to the back of the garden, ordered a beer and watched the music from the barstool with the banjo by my side, not really knowing what to expect. There were no microphones. It was all unplugged, which was how I liked it. The woman on stage, apparently Maya, was wiry and was wearing a black tank top which complimented her skinny arms. She had olive skin, dark frizzy hair and looked like any other *sabra*, the Hebrew slang word for native.

"Hey bro, is that a ukulele?" At my side was an older Israeli hippie in short jean cut-offs and a ponytail, holding a glass of red wine.

"It's a banjo," I sighed.

By this point, I was resigned to the fact that the banjo was not something that the Israeli people would take to as if it were part of their own history.

The woman on stage finished her song and people were clapping. I realized that she was motioning towards my general direction from the stage. I had no idea why. It was only me and this moshavnik at the bar, so she was signaling to either me or him. What was her name again? I seemed to remember Maya.

"You with that..." she paused for a second, with pursed lips, trying to conjure up some vocabulary word that was just on the tip of her tongue. "What is that?"

Before I was able to say anything, the *moshavnik* answered. *"Korim l'ze banjo."* It's called a banjo, he proclaimed to the entire crowd, like he was an instrument connoisseur. I saw this as progress.

Maya suddenly called me up to the stage. "Well, bring it here!" She motioned with her arm like I had just been a lucky game show contestant. The crowd collectively clapped in agreement.

"What shall we play?" Maya asked as I sat down next to her.

I had a moment of panic. Thus far, the banjo hadn't fared too well in Israel. It had terrorized Holocaust survivors and been rejected by teens intent on filling their otherwise peaceful homes with the sounds of death metal. Now I was sitting next to a beautiful woman with twenty people staring at me expectantly. What could I possibly play that could make this turn out okay?

"I know just the song," I told Maya. It had come to me like a vision of a burning bush. I would grace them with the Arik Einstein song, *"Ani Ve'Atah,"* whose lyrics translated as, "You and I will change the world."

I strummed the chords on my banjo and the crowd loved it. They began singing in unison.

Everyone belted out the words together with their arms around each other, like we were singing something as cherished as "American Pie," or "Blowin' in the Wind."

I had apparently found myself in some kibbutz-like alternate universe with my banjo, on a mountaintop stage, drinking homemade beer and singing with a beautiful *sabra* named Maya.

Later that night as I sat by the bar drinking and chatting with Danny's regular patrons, I silently hoped that something else would materialize with Maya. I was intrigued by her Israeli beauty but wasn't sure how she felt about me. She and her friends seemed like they were part of some cool secret club that I could never be a part of. They were all from Tel Aviv and artsy looking. It was hard to imagine them in army uniforms, holding weapons and manning checkpoints in occupied territory—which they must have had experience doing at some point in their lives. They were all wiry with long hair (the guys too), with necklaces and anklets. It was as if the sixties and had just returned—but in the Hebrew language.

Suddenly Maya appeared at my side. "We're going down to the beach. Do you want to come?"

"Um, sure." I was mystified. She really wanted me to come along?

"And you can bring your... " She paused for a second and kind of laughed. "Your banjo."

"What's so funny?"

"Atah Motek, ze hu." (You're a sweetie, that's all.)

She ruffled my hair with her hand, like I was a younger brother. The interaction saddened me a little, because it signaled the playfulness of a grade-school playground in her touch—the swing, the jungle gym, the sandbox and hide-and-go-seek. Nothing in that gesture, or her body language, gave me the slightest hope that there was any type of romantic possibility. I could tell that she was about ten years older than I was (which I hadn't noticed on stage). This made her all the more desirable.

"You'll ride with me."

I replied, *"Ein baya."* (No problem.)

In a chain of cars, we were like Arabian caravan scouts leading the group down the mountain along a windy path, crossing the highway, through the banana plants, under the train tracks and just past the sand dunes in her four-speed Peugeot that she handled effortlessly, barely feeling the space between the gears.

The stars were bright when we reached the beach. It was as if we had come to the end of a long journey and now it was time to make camp. There was something almost biblical about it. We were within sight of Mount Carmel and its cedars, the spot where Elijah the Prophet had allegedly ascended up to heaven in a chariot of fire. We were drinking bottles of red wine that we had taken from Danny's, seated around a fire pit we kindled with some logs and twigs that we had gathered in the dunes. We all sat cross-legged, smoking strawberry-flavored tobacco from her guitar player's water pipe, called a *nargileh*.

We were having the dumbest conversation too, an argument that would take longer to resolve than peace in the Middle East: where the best hummus in the country was to be found.

One guy said that it was in Rosh Pinna in the Galilee. Another insisted that his favorite was in the old city of Acre just an hour north of Haifa at some place called Sayeed's. No matter their preference, each person defended their choice in the same way: fingers clenched in little balls that were first held together at the chest and then shot outwards in a burst of Jewish frustration. This was the way all Israelis argued.

"What? Are you crazy? The best hummus in the country is at Nadima's in Wadi Nisnas," the drummer said, pointing in the direction of the city.

As authentic as my Israeli experience was that night, I could not enjoy it entirely as I was obsessed over Maya and how magnificent she seemed to me. The fact that she had patted me on the head like a sibling, the fact that she was wiser and more seasoned only made her that much more mysterious and desirable.

Maya didn't do anything that special to deserve this status. She was just being herself, laughing innocently at everyone with a wide smile. There were moments when we would make eye contact and I would look away immediately, for fear of exposing my desire, which I did and did not want her to be privy to all at the same time.

Eventually all of her friends went home and I was surprised that my unarticulated wish was granted: by some stroke of luck it was only the two of us left alone on that lonely sand dune, her car and the embers of the fire crackling like escaping fireflies. The wine had gone to both of our heads. I wanted to say something interesting, but I couldn't think of anything. We sat in silence for a while. Then I said the first thought that came to mind.

"Yesh lech kol yefa." (You have a pretty voice.)

Most of the night had been in Hebrew. Bits of English spilled into the conversations when I needed it. But this was the first time that she said something entirely in English, showing a firm grasp of the language. "Thank you, *sweetie.* You can speak English, I live in Brooklyn."

I was caught off guard. This was an interesting twist to the plot. "You live in New York?"

"Yes. With my boyfriend."

"Oh."

She lit a cigarette.

Then there was an awkward silence as I thought through what she had just said. I was a bit annoyed that she hadn't mentioned it before we came down from Ein Hod to the beach. Why else would she have consciously ended up alone with me here?

"I know what you're up to right now." She exhaled smoke as if being interrogated by a hardboiled detective. "Don't start with me."

We said nothing after that as we stared at the stars on her blanket. Later we packed up her Peugeot and as she was dropping me off, I hopped out and grabbed my banjo. I stuck my head back in through the passenger side window.

"Well, see you back in Brooklyn?" I heard myself saying. I didn't even live in New York, but I was already imagining our lives colliding again after she finally realized that I was the one for her.

"No, *matoki*. It was nice meeting you. *Yallah* bye."

I watched her drive off into the distance. The fading light of the tail pipe was like a star at the end of the universe, moving further and further away, just like the final fading spark of Elijah's chariot as he rode up to the Old Mighty.

I was invited many more times to play at Danny's Bar during my time in Haifa. I became the American with the banjo who played hillbilly music, but who also played a strange rendition of *"Ani Ve'Atah."* And every time that I did, I thought about Maya living her life somewhere in Brooklyn, New York.

CHAPTER FOUR

Living in Israel had one long-lasting effect: I fell in love with Hebrew for some reason. While I was there, somehow, the language of my heritage had magically passed from the ink of the Torah scroll in my eighth-grade minyan of pimply boys to the mouths of hot Israeli girls wearing army uniforms, donning M16s and eating ice cream cones in the streets of West Jerusalem on their days off from the base.

The language of the Tanakh (Hebrew Bible) and the siddur (prayer book) that I had learned in my youth was so different from the words I had encountered on the streets of Tel Aviv. Yet there were also words in the Israeli vernacular that were straight out of the sacred literature. The exit sign at the Kenyon Haifa Mall "Yetziah" shared the same word in the phrase *Yetziat Mitzrayim* (the exodus from Egypt). The word for vehicle (*rehev*) shared the same root for the Biblical word for chariot (*merkava*). And hilariously, *merkava* had been co-opted by the Israeli army for one of their classic tank models.

When I returned to Philly from Israel, I started seriously thinking about my future and all I wanted to do was study Hebrew. I knew my dad wouldn't be happy. Before my Quaker high school experience, I had first attended a Jewish day school as a kid, but I think his rationale was that when I was older he could kvell over me as the sole family member able to facilitate the occasional blessings at a Shabbat dinner or the family Seder, but that was the extent of it. My delving into Jewish things was supposed to have an expiration date: eighth grade graduation.

On a Sunday afternoon in our living room, I decided to break the news to my parents that I had been accepted to a master's program for Jewish education in New York City.

"This is the big one!" My father held his hands to his heart to make sure I really got the point he was trying to make: *The Big One* was family code for the impending heart attack that Dad was always waiting to have as a result of things not going his way. And the mere thought that I would become a professional Jew for a living was exactly his idea of things not going his way. (The last time I'd gotten this reaction, I'd come home from cross country practice in tenth grade and asked him, "Hey what do you think of my new hair color?" We'd all bleached our hair as a symbol of team unity.)

As far as Dad was concerned, I would be a pauper. He just couldn't wrap his mind around what it was exactly I wanted to do with such a degree in the first place.

"What does that even mean, Jewish education? So you go live on a kibbutz for a year and now you wanna be a rabbi?"

"I just like Hebrew."

"And what exactly will you do with Hebrew?"

"I guess I'll be a teacher."

"How are you going to make a living teaching Hebrew, Matthew?"

He went to the kitchen to pour himself a drink. He paced around the island and with every swirl of his glass of chardonnay he hoped for some nugget of wisdom that would repair the trajectory of my life. I knew what he was thinking. All his friends' kids were so much more successful than his own son. Jeff Stein was at Bear Stearns and had already saved enough to buy a condo in Chelsea. His younger brother Steve was at Wharton, finishing up his MBA and had a secured position at Wells Fargo in Center City, Philadelphia. Nathan Keller had just finished up at Emory and was about to start as a junior planner at Merrill Lynch. Even Henry Klein of all people was working on his JD and had plans to be a respectable public defender with the hopes of someday becoming partner at some firm in Fort Lauderdale or Tampa. And what did Ron Check's son want to do? He wanted to teach Hebrew.

"He's your son, not mine!" He pointed at Mom who was the only one who could talk Dad down from the mountain of scenarios that he was now crafting in his head, all of them ending in supporting me for the rest of my days on my poor teacher's salary.

Mom went to him and put her hand on his shoulder, patting him like a sidekick. "Ronnie, in Manhattan he'll meet a nice Jewish girl from Barnard—and marry rich!"

She turned his thoughts to something that he hadn't yet considered. I could be spending time in my father's most coveted neighborhood, the Upper East Side. It had his favorite hotels where he stayed during his business conventions: The Pierre and The Carlyle. It had his favorite overpriced restaurants and Bentleys too! Just a minute beforehand, he had imagined sending me rent-check-money for the rest of my days while I lived in some bombed-out tenement. But now, I could tell that he was imagining a scenario in which they would come to visit me and my Jewish-wife-to-be. Her name would be Sarah or Rachel, or Evelyn. She would be really thin, the way Mom was when they met, and he would make some snide comment about wanting to fatten her up with pasta. And Evelyn's father would be like my father in every way—a self-made businessman—except he would be named Art.

All of a sudden, it didn't seem like such a bad idea to buy me a beautiful one-bedroom apartment in the eighties on West End Avenue in a doorman building. And Art, since he was the type of classy guy who had box seats at Madison Square Garden and one of Dali's original melting clock paintings in the foyer of his Park Avenue penthouse with panoramic views, would surely offer to split the costs of the apartment that I had found with Evelyn. But Dad would argue over picking up the entire check after playing a round of golf together and hashing it out in the shvitz. "It's fine, Art, I got this, really. No, you can't even pay for the closing costs. I'm serious. You're gonna pay for the wedding, ya schmuck. That's what it takes to be the *machatunim*!" There would be laughter and pats on the back as they splashed aftershave on their cheeks next to each other in their adjacent sinks in the locker room. Eventually the most important thing of all would come along: Jewish grandchildren.

Or at least this is what I heard in the single sentence that Dad uttered: "Gail, get the Real Estate section! Trump Towers here we come!"

My introduction to the Big Apple was uneventful—and so was getting a place to live. I secured a beautiful apartment way uptown on 122nd and Claremont. The building had Gothic architecture and stained-glass windows in the lobby. The windows of my kitchen and bedroom looked into the courtyard of Riverside Church and every Sunday morning I woke up to the sound of bells.

In the beginning I barely left the enclave of Morningside Heights except for venturing downtown to the storied Wednesday night bluegrass jam at the Baggot Inn. The neighborhood included several seminaries, Bank Street College, the Manhattan School of Music, Barnard and Columbia University. It had the feel of a small university liberal arts town with its tree-lined streets, bookshops, cafes and multiple libraries, all of which I had access to because of an agreement between the schools.

I registered for classes and settled into a routine, going between courses on various types of Jewish literature, Hebrew and teaching pedagogy. While I enjoyed my schedule and loved New York, I immediately became aware of how expensive it was to live in the city. The fact that Dad was paying my way wore heavy on my conscience—especially because I knew that he would rather I was doing something different with my life. I heard from classmates that teaching at synagogue schools paid well. But the semester had already started and it seemed that all of the temples in the city had hired their staff. In desperation, I hoped that I might be able to at least give private Hebrew lessons, so I began trolling craigslist ads. Sadly, I only came across one relevant ad: "Teacher wanted to teach Hebrew on Saturday afternoons."

The ad had been placed by a group called The Chosen, which reminded me of the Chaim Potok novel of the same name, conjuring up for me the image of the boy in the yarmulke on the cover. Usually Jewish communities, whether official or not, had Hebrew in their titles like *bnai* this or *Kehillat* that. I decided to answer the ad anyway. It wasn't like I had lots to choose from.

I was excited when I arrived at the office on the West Side for an interview. The rabbi and his wife both turned out to be lovely people. I answered all of their questions with enthusiasm. I told them about my language proficiency, my time in Israel and showed them the instructional books that I would want them to order for the class. Then it was my turn to ask questions if I had any.

"So why the name?"

"Well, we are chosen," he said tautologically. I could tell by his body language that he was defending the honor of something, which I could identify with. After all we were Jews.

"I know what you mean, rabbi, but chosen for what?" I said with jazz hands, trying to be funny and referencing Tevye's opening monologue in *Fiddler on the Roof*.

They both sat there stoically not laughing at all. What the hell type of Jew didn't get a reference from *Fiddler*? Instead, the rabbi leaned forward with his hands clasped and whispered almost clandestinely, "We are chosen and Yeshua is our Messiah."

For the entirety of my life, I had heard Jews refer to "the Messiah" as *Meshiach*. And Yeshua? Who was that? I thought I had heard him incorrectly, so I asked him to clarify.

"Yeshua. The real name of Jesus. But we believe in Christ as..."

That word: Christ. Instead of hearing any more of his words, I suddenly heard a long and slow drum roll with reverb in the background, accompanied by a Baroque organ piece in a minor key with monks chanting some strange tome in Latin, something that started with the phrase *Spiritus Dominus*. I imagined Jesus (or Yeshua as they called him) as a longhaired hippie, his nice six-pack torso (that I always envied—even by working out at the gym, I simply couldn't get the abs that Jesus had), blood streaming down his forehead, wearing that diadem of thorns, eyes pointed toward heaven, pondering the thought that God had forsaken him. And suddenly I put it all together: These people were Jesus Jews!

"So what do you think? Do you want the job?"

Sure, I wanted to show my father that I could etch out a living doing what I loved. But even if I was feeling guilty that Dad paid my tuition and my rent, had life really come to this? Didn't I have any sense of self-worth or dignity? I had been raised on the stories of my ancestors having risked their lives to protect our traditions and our identity: the woman circumcising her babies in the forest in the face of Seleucid occupiers who had sacked the holy temple, the tannaitic sage saying his daily prayers at the risk of execution by Roman prefects. We had survived Christians, Visigoths and Nazis too. After all that, shouldn't I be spending my time teaching Hebrew to other Jews instead of evangelicals? I needed to walk out and continue to look for other jobs. I could even babysit if it came down to that.

"We'll pay you $200 an hour."

"When do I start?" I said without skipping a beat.

"So what was the first day of work like for you, Matt?"

"Well Phil, it was kind of like watching The Death of Klinghoffer.

Did you see it when you were alive? It came to Lincoln Center back in 2014? I mean you hadn't died yet."

"Absolutely not! John Adams stole my idea WHILE I was writing Operation Shylock, that rat bastard."

"Woah...I wasn't trying to drudge anything up there."

"Was it any good?"

"The dancing Palestinians with AK-47s was kind of fascinating."

The moment that I walked into The Chosen to start my new job was one of the stranger experiences of my life. The rabbi had just finished preaching in front of a piano that had an Israeli flag draped across it while people were lined up to do something that looked like taking communion as the pianist played Hatikvah, the national anthem of the State of Israel.

Half an hour later my students joined me in an adjacent room that smelled of burnt coffee urns and musky old library books. And suddenly I was having an authentic New York moment. If nothing else, this brand of religious faith had brought people together from all different colors and cultural backgrounds. The only white people, besides for the "rabbi" and his wife, were two evangelical-looking women with thick-rimmed glasses and salt and pepper hair. The one thing everyone had in common: They were all taking this class very seriously. There was a stiff formality to the room that I wasn't used to dealing with.

I hoped to lighten the mood and show them I was a laid-back teacher with a bit of humor. I told them my name was Matthew and then explained why. "I once complained to my father that even though I'm a Jew, he named me after an apostle. My father answered back, 'An apostle. Really? Which one?'"

I stood there like a comedian, waiting for the punch line to sink in. But they didn't show me that Jewish smile so appreciative of irony. Instead, they looked at me with all the sincerity in the world, as if waiting for a spiritual nugget of wisdom that had yet to come.

"So you are our apostle and Yeshua has sent you to teach us!" Beatrice, a lady in her fifties, attempted to interpret what I had just said for the class.

"Yes!" said George from the other end of the table. "You are our teacher!" Everyone else nodded their heads earnestly.

Even though the class didn't display much of a sense of humor, on that first day I learned how well meaning they were as they diligently pronounced letter after letter of the Hebrew alphabet like they were soldiers in boot camp.

"Everyone say '*chet*' with me."

"*Het*," they all said in unison, making the sound of the letter H.

"No, not *het. Chet!*"

"*Het*," they all repeated.

I put down my piece of chalk. "George, pretend that you are stuffed up and have a really bad cold."

"Um, okay?"

"What is the noise that you make when you attempt to clear your throat?"

He paused for a second and thought about it. He touched his neck and made the glottal sound, "Ehem!"

"Very good! Now everyone do the same thing, just add a T at the end of the phrase."

"*Chet!*" It sounded like a chorus of karate students learning how to chant their kata and attempting to graduate from their white belts. But it worked. They all smiled.

"Very good, everyone. Make sure to never say a word with the letter *chet* in while you have food in your mouth." It wasn't even funny, but everyone burst into laughter at the tables. I had broken the ice.

I didn't feel comfortable telling people in my life where I was going and what I was teaching. It was my own little secret. But that is what I did on Saturday afternoons during the period of my life when I was working on a master's degree in Jewish education. When all my other classmates were teaching children in synagogue schools or making sermons as rabbinic interns or chanting *musaf* as cantorial soloists at storied institutions of the greater metropolitan area, I was teaching Hebrew to people who had wafers in their bellies after taking communion to the sound of Hatikvah.

During those first weeks I realized that my Jesus Jew students loved Hebrew more than anyone I had ever met. In my experience most American Jews hated learning our eternal language—it was like pulling teeth. Even in my biblical grammar course, all of us rolled our eyes as the professor wrote out and described the rules of *nikkud* (vocalization) on the blackboard. But my room was full of Jesus Jews—they were all like a determined bunch of math nerds. They took notes and asked penetrating questions that challenged me to really explain the minutiae of things. They were able to read the words in the exercises that I assigned. They remembered the vocabulary too.

I realized they were ready for the banjo.

I brought it to class one day. But as I took the banjo out of its case, it occurred to me that I hadn't fully thought through what I would actually sing with them. For a moment, I considered playing "Little Maggie" or "Molly and Tenbrooks" but soon thought better of it. There was no educational value in these songs. Was there such a thing as a Jesus Jew repertoire? I didn't know. All I could think of was the lone song that I knew how to play in Hebrew: *Ani Ve'Atah*.

I faced my class with the banjo like I was at an open mic. "I once played this on a mountaintop in Israel."

"On the Sea of Galilee?" George asked in excitement, obviously having not heard me correctly.

"No, a mountaintop. You know, like the sermon?"

Everyone stared at me, not getting my joke.

"Okay, anyway, the words are very simple". I asked them to repeat the words after me.

Even after a few repetitions, they were still stumbling through them so I decided to write out the song on the blackboard. Then I began to strum the opening A minor chord as everyone attempted to sing the melody along with me. They struggled but loved it anyway.

"It means, 'You and I, we'll change the world.'"

Suddenly all of my Jesus Jew students' faces lit up. I guess it was the message of the song. They stumbled through the chorus again, but this time with a newfound fervor. A few put arms around each other and began swaying back and forth. I thought the action was cheesy but the movement turned out to be contagious. They included me in what became one big circle, like at a summer camp bonfire. It was our "Kumbaya" moment.

For me something shifted in that moment. I realized that what I was doing at The Chosen was outside of my comfort zone, but it was also a combination of the things that I loved most. I was speaking Hebrew and playing the banjo.

After that day, I felt strangely like one of them. I even showed up at the end of services, to eat with them at Kiddush (I can't believe that's what they called it, but they did), making small talk as if it were my own community.

On one of these days a small, scraggly and bald congregant named Gary approached me as I was picking from one the platters of poppy seed bagels and lox.

"I have a problem."

"What type of problem?"

"A theological one. I heard that you're studying to be a rabbi or something."

"No, just education."

"Well anyway…I've got questions, and you seem to be knowledgeable."

I was flattered by the solicitation, someone asking me for advice. I was making a difference—one Jesus Jew at a time. Gary lived downtown, which I hadn't explored much of yet because I was so new in the city. I suggested that we meet at Caffe Reggio on MacDougal Street (my parents had always talked about getting coffee there in the seventies).

I brought him three different books on Jewish theology that had inspired me personally, which I thought would provide some examples of my own theological palette: Mordecai Kaplan's *Judaism as a Civilization*, A. J. Heschel's *God in Search of Man* and the collected essays of Ahad Ha'am, my favorite Zionist ideologue. When I spotted him walking through the door, I smacked my palm down upon Kaplan's seminal tome, like I was a witness ready to testify to the truth I'd learned about God. "So I was thinking about a couple of different people for you to read."

"I lied about the reason that I asked to meet with you."

"Okay." I was a little disappointed as I had been looking

forward to serving as a mentor of sorts, embarking on all sorts of fun theological discussions. Maybe I had overwhelmed him with my reading material.

"I was wondering." He paused for a second. "I was wondering if you wanted to join my gangbang fraternity."

"Your what?" I wasn't sure I'd heard him right.

"You know...a gangbang. A few friends and I get together, get a hooker and we take turns having sex with her. I was wondering if you wanted to join us. I'm the club president. It's all about the high five." He put his hand up, waiting for me to slap it. I simply couldn't return the gesture. One hand was still holding my coffee mug, the other was spread across the cover of a canonical piece of 20th century Jewish literature, written by the father of the Recon-structionist movement.

"The high five?" I repeated as a question.

"Yeah. And we have theme nights too." He put his hand up again, waiting for a second returned high five that also never came. I was suddenly afraid that I was going to contract the STD version of Ebola if I touched him.

"Theme nights?"

"Yep. Taco Tuesdays and Falafel Wednesdays."

I imagined a bunch of bros rooting one of their friends on while he rammed someone from behind only to "high five" everyone after finishing while his cock was still wet and dripping with the diseased stink of sin's love sluice. All of this combined with the scent of Curry-in-a-Hurry. I didn't think that the olfactory system was meant to be subjected to all that in a closed space. I hoped that they had ventilation.

"I thought you'd be into it." Gary ordered a latte but his former confidence was gone. He was like a weasel that had just been caught in a Raymond Chandler story.

"Really? Why?"

"Well...you know...the banjo."

Apparently the banjo was cosignatory with sexual depravity now? He was now reducing my beloved instrument to a crack whore? I realized that we would need to treat this interaction like a teacher having a one-night stand with his student—we would never speak of it again.

"Anyway Phil, that was the first and the last time that I was a handshake away from agreeing to take turns having sex with a woman with a bunch of other dudes on a random weeknight while eating street-side Halal food."

"You mean a high five away."

"Ha. You're right."

"Didn't you consider the artistic potential here, Matt? As much as I love your Spanish love song and your versions of Israeli folk music, wasn't this an opportunity for another project like "Gangbang Breakdown" or something of the sort?"

"No, Phil. I left Caffe Reggio thinking that I had met someone who probably kept the gurgling spittle of a Nepalese sex worker in a Dixie cup like an aging wine ready to drink during an epic gangbang session, with a straw."

"Been there, Matt."

Instead of being relieved that I at least had some employment during graduate school (albeit he didn't know who I was teaching), my father was mostly preoccupied with the lack of women in my life.

"How about the girls, Matthew? Do you have a girlfriend yet?" He still had his heart set on meeting Art and Evelyn sometime in the very near future.

"Not yet," I would tell him time and time again.

"Come on, talk! Fess up! What's her name?"

"Dad, I'm really not seeing anyone at all."

"Just wear a rubber okay. You've gotta protect the family jewels."

"Dad!"

"What? I'm just saying!"

I did take a few girls out on dates. I just didn't tell my parents. They had first names like Rachel, Tamar, Talia and Sarah. They had last names like Katz, Cohen, Feinberg and Levy. They were all lovely and all liked me back. I even slept with a few of them. But no one really piqued my interest long term. No one ascended from the primordial soup of otherness, darkness and intensity like Paulette, Isabella and Maya—characteristics that ignited something real and savory within me and inspired music for reasons I could not explain.

One October night, I was sitting across from a pretty girl on the subway with brown curls that for some reason made me think of sausage links. She was wearing a tan trench coat and was dozing off. Her laptop was about to fall from her lap. She awoke with a head bob and grabbed it before it hit the floor of the car.

"Tired?" I blurted out for some reason.

The girl smiled and chuckled. "Yes. A bit, I suppose." She had an English accent. She looked at my instrument inquisitively. "What is that?" she asked.

The train arrived at Christopher Street in the West Village. The doors opened and I got up to leave. "It's a banjo."

"A what?" she asked innocently. I walked off into the night

annoyed. She would never know. Most instances were like this one. I would use the banjo as a reason to strike up a conversation, and most women insulted my beloved instrument instead of being drawn in by it.

"Are you being metaphorical here? Your beloved instrument, Matt?"

"Now that you mention it, I actually did want to talk about my penis again."

"Can't wait."

As if to ensure that I would never get a girlfriend, I discovered a bump on my penis one morning when I was showering. It was a white fleshy-looking fellow, staring at me as if to say, "Hi, you don't know me, but I'm gonna be here for a while!" I brushed my finger across it, hoping it would go away. I was suddenly seized with a kind of anxiety I had never known before. Every five minutes I would get up and go check myself. The bump was still there every time.

"You have an STI," the doctor at the Columbia Medical Center told me.

"What's that? VD?"

"The proper terminology these days is sexually transmitted infection, an STI. And yes, you have genital warts."

Warts? Ugh. Avoid-the-clap-Jimmy-Dugan! I thought of Allen.

Yes, I had been with a couple of girls since arriving in the city. But it wasn't like I solicited total strangers on the street corner and then barebacked it in some cobblestoned alleyway while being slapped in the face because I liked that sort of thing. I had done it in a bed, with consent, with protection and then offered whoever it was that I *shtupped* coffee and eggs in the morning before kicking her out so that I could get back to my homework.

Regardless of who gave it to me, I was now in the category of the sexually depraved because I was going to be alone for the rest of my life with my new little companion, a tiny, white, fleshy friend that I would now name Lucky, like Dad's childhood Beagle who was run over by a truck.

"Matthew, eighty percent of Americans have HPV. If you've had three sexual partners, you've got it. You can practically look in someone else's general vicinity and contract it." He was right. I was proof. Gary Gangbang had apparently wafted it towards my nether regions—that flesh-taco-eating fuck. I might as well call him up and join the gangbang fraternity now. For sure I'll be picking up the tacos as some sort of hazing ritual for my first night.

"Did it inspire you to write new material?"

"Would it inspire you, Phil? I was empty of inspiration! Nothing does that more to you than finding out that your cock is just as syphilitic as Benjamin Franklin's by the time he was suffering from kidney stones in a Parisian whorehouse in his mid seventies."

"How do we treat it?" I asked Dr. Tate.

"Many people use a prescribed ointment. But we can also burn it off with acid. That will take a few seconds. It will turn brown into a scab, but it won't scar."

"Doc, give me the acid."

"Are you sure?" Dr. Tate seemed surprised by my immediate request. I felt like a wounded knight asking his squire to pull an arrow from his shoulder and cover up the open flesh wound with a searing flame.

"Yes. I want it off. Cut me!"

"Matt, there's no knife."

"JUST TAKE IT OFF. PLEASE!"

With blue latex gloves, he opened a small apothecary bottle and squeezed a few drops on me from an eyedropper. I watched as the liquid turned Lucky from fleshy white, to a dark brown, and then suddenly and astonishingly, to black.

"Ah, fuck!" I shouted. The sensation passed almost immediately. I pulled my pants up.

"You might have more," Dr. Tate said. "Don't worry, it will run its course. Please come in for a checkup every three weeks. It should go away soon. And always use a condom."

I didn't go every three weeks. I went three times a week, because I had Avoid-the-clap-Jimmy-Dugan. I shaved myself to make sure I wasn't getting bumps all around my groin area. Another bump appeared on the tip and then one at the base of the shaft. I was like a kid with acne but it was on my Johnson—a diseased cock. It was long before the selfie, but I photographed it, just to remind myself that there were better days ahead. And so I continued to return to the doctor that entire season. By late November I wasn't showing any new bumps and Dr. Tate attempted to wean me off of leaching to him in desperation.

"You don't have to come every week," Dr. Tate said. "You haven't had a bump in a month. It's a good sign that you're in the clear. Just make sure to use a condom."

I saw things in a different light though. I had been walking around the streets of Morningside Heights with my Hebrew books and my banjo and my spotted member—a broken man of twenty-five. And it wasn't because I had betrayed my ideals by going to law school or med school or business school, or God forbid because I took golf lessons in order to become a seasoned and respectable professional with a 401K and a mortgage. It was *davka ha'hefech*—

precisely the opposite. It was because I followed my dreams. It was because I was teaching gangbanging Jesus Jews and had somehow contracted a fatal disease from Nancy Rotten-crotch wherever she was! I failed. I couldn't even protect the family jewels. Maybe I should just join the Hari Krishnas and shave my head. If anything it would match the shaved nether regions.

"Please stop coming," Dr. Tate insisted in December. I'd had no symptoms in a month and a half.

"Just check for me, doc. PLEASE. Last time, I promise. I just need to know that I'm finally beating this disease." I pulled my pants down without him even asking, waiting for him to inspect.

"You're not diseased, Matt. It's just an STI. It's not cancer. I release you. Just use a condom and tell your sex partners. Get on with your life."

But I knew the score. It was the mark of Cain. VD just doesn't go away. It's always there—like antisemitism. Zionist-loving genital warts don't exist. There are only Nazi warts, with perfectly coiffed genital wart Nazi hair. I was going to be alone for the rest of my life.

All of the apocalyptic thoughts that I had been having about my spotted dick were suddenly forgotten when I passed through the waiting room. I noticed a girl sitting there leafing through a magazine. I was sure I recognized her. It took me a minute to re-member. It was the girl with the sausage curls from that night on the subway, the one with the English accent who was falling asleep. She had the same tan trench coat and the same laptop that she had almost dropped.

"Still tired?" I asked.

She looked up, wondering who this stranger was and what he was saying. But then, as if a piece of a puzzle was finally set in its place, she recognized me. Her hands were folded on her lap, her legs crossed.

"You're the…"

"From the 1 train, Friday night, headed downtown."

"And that is how Johanna and I met, Phil. The rest is commentary."

CHAPTER FIVE

Just like I was meant to play the banjo, I would come to wonder if I was meant to meet Johanna Kahn. Perhaps she had been always waiting in the wings and women like Paulette, Isabella and Maya were simply some collective warm-up act. *Was this serendipity?* I asked myself. After all, New York was the type of place where these things happened.

I knew nothing about this new person in my life other than the fact that she dozed off on subway cars and had an accent. But there was something that drew me to her. That day at the doctor's office, I was trembling so badly when I asked for her number, I nearly dropped my cell phone as I walked away.

A week later, I met her and her friends for drinks downtown in Nolita at a little restaurant called Epistrophy on Mott Street. It was a dark corridor and I imagined that decades earlier, prior to the crack epidemic, it had probably been Moshe Klein's shoe repair. Her friends were all seated in the back with glasses of red wine in the same place where I imagined that good old Moshe had sat decades before, lathing his leather shoes day in and day out, in the shop that he built with his two hands, while his wife Shandel pestered him for having too much gas because of the sauerkraut he ate every night.

Johanna motioned for me to come over and sit next to her. She kissed me on both cheeks. "Hello, *Bello*."

I immediately felt as if I were in one of the scenes from the black and white Bob Dylan movie, *Don't Look Back* with Donovan and Joan Baez. Her friends all appeared to be artsy and intellectual—donning colorful sweaters, scarves and large-rimmed glasses. It was like an exclusive party that banjo-playing Jesus-Jew-teaching, Hebrew *grammarniks* like myself from the uptown did not easily gain access to.

They were mid conversation about the symbolism in the Spanish movie *Pan's Labyrinth* that had come out that year and were throwing out terms like "magical realism" and "mise-en-scène." They were mysterious and interesting and intimidating.

"Do you have any favorite *films*, Matt?" Sophie asked me innocently. She was a Dutch writer, working on her Ph.D.

I kept wanting to insert a joke into the conversation about how when the word "Dutch" was placed before any other noun, it sounded like you were referring to a sex position. Dutch puppy. Dutch candy. Dutch sneakers. But I wasn't sure how this would go over with this mise-en-scène crowd.

"I like *film noir*?" I asked, wracking my brain for some erudite movie references in the event that they wanted me to expand.

Someone mentioned Lauren Bacall in *The Big Sleep* and then they started talking about Hitchcock. It wasn't that I couldn't keep up—it was the way that one of the guys said the word *"milieu"* that just seemed so over the top.

"It's the French word for 'setting,' Matt."

"I know, Phil. I just always thought it sounded like someone dry heaving, like after you have one piña colada too many and there you are in the bathroom."

"So why were you in the doctor's office?" Johanna asked me when there was a lull in the conversation.

"Blood work," I lied, not quite yet ready to tell her about Lucky and his little visit to my immune system.

"Oh, me too. I also needed to get a prescription for malaria. I'm on my way to Kenya." She explained that she was working on a master's in international diplomacy and the following month she was going on a mission sponsored by Columbia University with UN Secretary General Kofi Annan.

I wanted to know how long she'd be gone but didn't want her to notice my concern. Instead I said, "Oh, Africa," like it was Queens or the Bronx or Staten Island. "I almost went to Tangiers the year I studied abroad in Madrid but never made it," I said, failing to sound remotely interesting. Maybe that's because it wasn't true. Friends of mine had gone, but I had never had any desire to visit. The only thought in my head when I heard the word "Africa" was angry loinclothed-machete-wielding rebels, raiding villages full of children with dysentery. Did they even have toilet paper there? Wasn't that the place where you never touched your food with your left hand because that was the hand reserved for wiping?

"I've never been to Morocco but would adore the chance to

go," Johanna said, putting her hands to her heart. "If you ever go to Morocco, YOU HAVE TO see Mustafa Ali in Marrakesh." Apparently, he was a friend of hers from Paris who now lived there.

He could have been Mufasa from *The Lion King* for all I cared. Normally I would have mocked an accent like hers. But this time I was drawn to it instead, and marveled at how it matched her deep brown eyes, her railroad thinness, the sausage curls of her hair and her apparent desire to gobble up the whole world with phrases like "Mustafa Ali." She almost whispered it clandestinely: "Mustafa Ali, at the French Institut of Marrakesh with no E. He's a darling. Don't forget it." As she said this, she tapped me on the thigh, as if she were a secret agent telling me things I shouldn't know.

"Mustafa and I used to dance tango in the 9th. That's where I first learned to dance. Do you dance, Matt?"

"The hora," I said without thinking.

She laughed at my idiocy as she sipped from her glass of wine. So she liked me and my obvious lack of sophistication. This was good.

"I've danced the hora many a time. My mother is Jewish."

"Un-fucking-believable Matt."

"I know. Right, Phil?"

It took me a second to process everything. But once I did, I realized that this girl I had met on the subway and bumped into at the doctor's office where I was being treated for VD was more than just a beautiful and intellectual woman, potentially harboring some secret nugget of wisdom to offer from the depths of her European mystique. She was more than a tango-dancing world traveler who had allowed Ebola babies to suckle on her nipples in the darkest depths of the African Sahara. She wasn't just a machete-fleeing traveler who had made love to Mustafa Ali at the French Institut with no E of Marrakesh! The woman I had just met was Jewish. If we were Polish and it had been 1943, we'd be on a train headed for Auschwitz together.

Many drinks and several hours later, I walked Joanna to her place. Standing at her front door, I counted on saying our goodbyes, but to my immense surprise, she invited me up to her apartment.

"Why don't you come up for a night cap?"

"Me?" I was amazed. I didn't realize that I might have passed some test of coolness.

"Yes. My roommate is staying at her boyfriend's. Come on up." She grabbed my hand like a parent urgently taking hold of a child and coercing him to make the departing school bus.

While she uncorked a random bottle of red, I perused her collection of books in the living room: *The Politics of Dispossession* and *Orientalism* by Edward Said, *Palestinian Identity* and *The Iron Cage* by Rashid Khalidi, *Drinking the Sea at Gaza* by Amira Hass and *Selected Poems* by Mahmoud Darwish. I knew these writers. I had read some of them as well. And they were quite unlike the Zionist-friendly writers I was used to spending my time with. I was confused. Just an hour earlier she had said that she was Jewish.

"I see that you've found my books." She approached me at her bookshelf and handed me a glass of wine.

"I thought you were Jewish?" I asked, still fingering through them and stopping at the red, green and white flag on the spine of Khalidi's *Palestinian Identity*.

"My mum is Jewish and my dad is Muslim. It's complicated."

And so it was. The only thing she was missing was a Fatah soccer jersey.

"I've just always been fascinated with Palestine. It's a beautiful country and has an amazing culture." She looked out the window down onto the street corner as if she were pining for it.

"I've been to Ramallah," I said.

"Oh? Don't you just adore it, especially in the spring?"

She was the first person that I had ever met who'd said that she *adored* a Palestinian city. But for some reason, everything that she said was okay. In fact, I realized that she could have said anything and I would have thought it was some lyric from an Arabian epithalamion. It didn't matter if there was a hint of anti-Zionist sentiment here. Cupid's arrow had found my *tuchus*.

"I adore *you*," I told her.

"You say the strangest things, Mr. Check."

"Says the girl that likes Ramallah in the springtime."

She laughed and I was relieved to know I hadn't made a mistake. And so I did it—I kissed Johanna Kahn.

"That was lovely, Mr. Check," she said, pulling away from me.

The excitement of the moment, however, was replaced by my anxiety about telling her about my VD. I hadn't had a bump in month in a half and according to Dr. Tate I could *shtup* as long as I used a condom. Conflicting thoughts still entered my head anyway.

It was as if a harpsichord had begun to play in the background and a mini Dr. Tate was on my left shoulder as an angel with flapping wings, whispering a sonnet in my ear: "Tell her Matt / ethics are key / If she likes thee doth / she'll sleep with thee." But then from the other shoulder, in a devil's costume, with Poseidon's spear and the whiskers of a Chinese ancient, was none other than Gary Gangbang himself munching on a taco—it must have been Tuesday in the ninth circle of hell. "Bang her Matt / Don't talk of

VD / Once thou finish / leave a round for me!"

I couldn't listen to Gary. I had to be straight with her.

"I have to tell you something," I said dramatically.

"Okay?"

"Well, I don't want to be assuming that we're going to sleep with each other, but I have HPV and can't have sex right now. But I'd still love to cuddle."

"You used the phrase 'to cuddle'?"

"Yes, Phil. And immediately regretted it."

"You're an idiot." She pulled me to her and continued to kiss me, as if pretending not to have heard me, though I knew she had. My lack of tact was the night's theme for sure. And yet strangely she liked all of it.

For me it was just more proof that something significant was happening to me. It was just like I was meant to play the banjo and meant to love the Hebrew language. It was as if Johanna Kahn had always been waiting in the wings, ready to step onto the stage of my existence.

☆ ☆ ☆

If anyone was happier than me at the news that I had finally met a girl, it had to be my father. Given my dating track record since I had moved to New York, I was beginning to suspect he thought I was gay.

"A girl? Hold on. Don't move. Gail! Your baby's on the phone! He's got a GIRLFRIEND!"

"She's not my girlfriend. I just..."

"Hold on, son. I'm gonna put you on speakerphone so we can

have a threeway."

I hated when he said that.

"Hi, Matt."

"Hi, Mom."

"So what's her name, son?"

"Johanna."

"What does she do?"

"She's in grad school."

"So she's smart, just like your mother. Meant to be!" My dad was probably looking at my mother when he said that. "Where'd you meet?"

"The subway and then ran into her at the doctor's office," *where I was being treated for spotted dick.*

"*Really* meant to be, son! Where is she from?"

"England."

There was a pause on the other end of the line. When my father spoke again, all the excitement was gone from his voice. "British? Forget it!" His first wife had been from London. "She'll cook you peas and Brussels sprouts."

"Dad, she's Jewish."

"So when do we get to meet her?"

I decided not to mention the fact that her father was Muslim. There would be plenty of time for that later on.

☆ ☆ ☆

Over the next week my father's words repeated themselves back to me: *So when do we get to meet her?* In my head we were having brunch at the Carlyle already. Dad would get eggs Benedict, Mom a single poached egg with salmon and asparagus, and Johanna would exotically order a parfait, causing my father to bring out his trademark sarcasm about not eating enough. Mom would then kick him under the table, giving us all a good laugh, just in time for my father's announcement that the wedding could happen at Greenacres (our family's country club in Lawrenceville, New Jersey) as long as Johanna's parents were willing to fly in.

Though before any of this could happen, first I would have to make her my girlfriend.

Unfortunately, the same wave of intimidation that I had experienced the night at Epistrophy came over me as I crossed the threshold of her apartment for a party she had invited me to.

It was as if Sophie and her French film boyfriend had been cloned exponentially for a European bohemian gala. The party was filled with artsy-looking types wearing tight clothing and speaking foreign languages. I felt as if I were in some combination of a scene from *Moulin Rouge!* and a strange postmodern Biblical re-interpretation of the Tower of Babel.

I made my way through the crowd, catching snippets of dialogue until finally I spotted Johanna. She was wearing a white dress with an open back and had a colorful silk neckerchief draped around her neck, reminding me of Maria from *West Side Story*.

But something was off about the scene in front of me. She hadn't seen me yet, but she was standing a little too close to the man next to her. The fingers of his right hand rested upon her elbow ever so subtly. They were talking in French while laughing about some private *pensée* that I was not privy to. I felt like leaving even before putting my banjo down when Johanna saw me and motioned for me to come to her.

"Bello, you came." She administered a kiss upon each of my cheeks. She seemed happy to see me at least. That was a win, wasn't it? Maybe there was no reason for me to be so suspicious.

"Yes, here," I said, handing her the bottle of red wine that I had bought down the street.

"I want you to meet my friend Manu. He's in my politics of dispossession class this semester."

Manu? Was that even a real name? It sounded like it was short for manure.

"Is Manu short for something?"

"Yes. Manuel."

"I'm Matt, short for Matthew."

For a second there was an awkward silence and no one knew what to say.

"You two have a chat," said Johanna as she walked away with my bottle. "I'm going to open this and catch up with Francesca. She's a is a dear friend from Milan!"

"Ah, Milano," Manu said as Johanna walked away.

I had just met him and was already envious of the way he said *"Milano."* He mouthed the word with a touch of ennui, like it was as familiar as West Palm Beach.

I asked him the first thing that came to mind. "So where are you from?"

"Liechtenstein." He pronounced the "ch" gutturally and the s as if it were "sh": *Liechhhhtenshhhhtein.* Of course, he was from that small and exotic Alpine Germanic country that sounded like something between a terminal illness and the camp where Nazi doctors performed experiments.

"Working on any interesting papers right now?"

"One about Palestine," he said as if it were some badge of honor that he got to wear. He looked at me with intense eyes, daring me, as if I represented part of the collective desire to rip that badge from some beautifully knitted alpaca sweater that he bought in Cuzco and wore in his lodge at his alpine ski resort—the one he took from my great grandparents—whilst visiting with Mummy and Daddy every Christmas, sitting by the fireplace and drinking sherry after eating a ham!

"I've been to Ramallah."

"Charming." He sipped his Montepulciano and seemed completely uninterested in. "I met the chairman a few times myself before he fell ill and Israeli tanks rolled into the *Mukataa*," Manu said, referring to Yasser Arafat and the compound where he lived out the final years of his life.

"Wow, you pronounce the sound of the *qopf* in Mukataa amazingly!" I really was amazed. He obviously had taken some Arabic lessons.

Confused by my comment, he decided to size me and my banjo up and down with his blue eyes. "So what do you do?"

"Me, oh, I'm a Hebrew teacher. I also play bluegrass," I said tapping my banjo case.

He stared at it in amazement. I watched his face turn from intrigue to horror, as if there had been a hairy mole staring at him in a mirror messing up the perfection he'd achieved with his coiffed blond hair. He was staring at a sticker of an Israeli flag on my case.

There was another awkward silence between the two of us but by now I had made my peace with it. As much as I resented his presence, I could see why someone European and sophisticated like Johanna would like him, besides the fact that their political ideologies were in sync. He was sleek like a river otter, with Übermensch blond hair and blue eyes. He looked healthy. He probably ate yoghurt and muesli for breakfast while reading his *Paris Review* or *Le Monde* or *Der Spiegel*, or the *Palestine Times* that he learned how to read in actual Arabic while studying at Birzeit University, which was later perfected by hanging out with Arafat at the Mukataa.

I was sure he had a bikini wax because he was the type of European guy who would get away with one of those teeny speedo swimsuits. He probably shaved his butthole too. He probably asked the women he slept with to slip the tip of a lubricated pinky up his corn hole to tickle the prostate because he was the type of guy that was *open* to that kind of thing. If it was going to be Johanna later that night, his roast-beefy foreskin would surely be involved somehow as well. *Ugh, smegma.*

More than anything though, he was smart and handsome in a classical sort of way that I could never be. He reminded me of how my cloistered, banjew life in Morningside Heights was so different from this downtown bohemia I had found myself in. I was now a lonely and forlorn fig—sweet but all shriveled up. I might as well be tossed to the wind to be eaten by some mother possum and her babies on the side of the road. I wanted to leave the party even though I had barely just arrived.

"It was nice to meet you, Manu."

"You as well."

And with that, I walked out the door of Johanna's apartment without even saying good-bye.

That night I turned to what I knew best: the banjo and whiskey. It was as if I was the protagonist in a really pathetic and sad country song. Fortunately I knew of a bluegrass jam happening nearby so I took a short walk to Mercer Street in Greenwich Village. Making my way through a packed apartment, I beelined it for the kitchen, found a handle of Jim Beam and poured myself a whiskey.

A woman entered the kitchen with her fiddle and bow in one hand and a glass of white wine in the other. It took me a moment to place her, but then I remembered: Mara Lae Lee. She was Chinese-American, raised in Utah and though she had recently moved to the city to pursue her career as a classical violinist, she loved bluegrass and Appalachian fiddle music. We had met a few weeks before at a friend's birthday party on the Lower East Side where she was wearing an elegant long black dress as if she were ready to step onto the symphony stage. Now she was wearing jeans and a flannel button-down shirt.

"Hey, Matt Check!"

"Hi, Mara!"

"Come on, play a tune with me." She tugged at my arm with the whiskey.

"Little Maggie" seemed like a good song to get us started. She placed her glass of wine next to my whiskey and set her fiddle at the meeting point of her chin and her neck.

I zipped into the opening lick, going from A to G, back to A and up to E, while Mara chucked along with her bow. As we sang the first verse together, a group of drinkers crowded around us, rooting us on like we were some famous jazz duo.

When I got to the line, "She's drinking away her troubles by courtin' another man," I thought of Johanna and Manu—in a primordial soupy Palestinian sea of smegma, of course.

Mara and I played a few more fiddle tunes together in the kitchen: "Big Sciota," "Red Haired Boy" and "Angeline the Baker." I poured us both a round of whiskey, half knowing that I was up to no good. I had one more, and a beer. I fetched Mara some more white wine from the fridge. Our playing lilted into giggling as the booze set in.

Later that night I walked her to the bus stop on the corner of Mercer and East 8th Street, where we waited for the bus headed towards the East Village. By that point we were both pretty loose. There was a moment during that walk that my thoughts turned from a somewhat innocent interaction with Mara to an all-of-a-sudden vendetta against Johanna. Even though I hadn't actually been rejected in the real world in any explainable way, I had a certain something to settle, and Mara would be the way I would go about it.

"I'm going to kiss you," I slurred.

"Do you want to come see my apartment?" she asked.

"Yes." It was that easy. I didn't even need to do any convincing.

"I'm not sleeping with you though."

"Oh good. We can just cuddle," I blurted out without thinking.

"That's the second time you told a woman that you wanted to cuddle in the story so far Matt."

"I know, Phil. Believe me, I know."

"And she still…"

"Yes! She still invited me over. I'm kind of happy that she didn't want to sleep with me though, given the VD convo and all."

I was dozing off with Mara by my side when suddenly my phone buzzed. It was a call, not a text from Johanna. My heart fluttered, like a flounder being yanked at by some fisherman up above the water's surface. "Hello?" I whispered.

"Hello, Bello," she whispered back. "Where art thou?"

"Asleep."

"Why don't you come sleep with me?" I was confused. I checked the time and it was seven-a-fucking-clock-in-the-morning. I said the first thing that came to mind. "Where is Manu?"

"What? Why would you ask that?"

"I don't know. You both seemed to like each other."

"Come downtown," she said. It was as if my comment wasn't even relevant. I could hear in her voice that I had been wrong, that Manu meant nothing to her and that she probably had wanted me to stay at the party. Perhaps it wasn't over. Perhaps there was no reason to have broken up with her in my head after all.

Mara stirred and rolled over and pecked at me like a butterfly up and down my clavicle, making a chirping sound.

"Who's that?" asked Mara.

"Who is *that*?" asked Johanna.

Mara took my phone from me, closed it and placed it on the night table. "Hold me," she said, falling back to sleep right away.

I checked my messages after Mara dozed back off to sleep. There was a text from Johanna. "Well, I hope you're having a GREAT time with whomever you're shagging this morning, Mr. Check."

It was at that moment that my feelings went from desire to necessity—a need to be with Johanna that I don't know I will ever quite sort out for myself.

"Whatever the reason, Phil, I came up with the lines to the first song I wrote about Johanna Kahn while I was in bed with another woman. When I played and sang the song for the first time, it felt as if it had been

sleeping within me, waiting to wake up and like I was always meant to sing those lines:'Back to sleep my love / that's the way it ought to be / back to sleep my love / it may not be fate, it might not be destiny.'"

"The only thing you've been destined for so far in your book is a peppered schlong."

"Oh fuck you, Phil."

"Finally, I'm getting to see the real Matt Check."

Later that day at my apartment, I recorded the song on my computer with a banjo, guitar, three-part harmonies and a drum track, as if I had a full band to back me up. I sent it to Johanna, hoping that it would evoke what I was experiencing: that I had to be with her. She called soon after.

"Did you write that song for me?"

"Yes."

"You are insanely ridiculous."

I would come to love the way that she said "ridiculous"—that and the way she expressed her adoration for Marrakesh and Ramallah on the first night that we kissed. Moments like these I will eternally cherish about Johanna Kahn.

CHAPTER
SIX

There was more than physical intimacy when it came to Johanna, something more subtle playing itself out that I found difficult to articulate because it hadn't happened to me before. I was catapulted into some higher realm, in which we were fixated on each other's existence and nothing else. I don't know if it was love, obsession, or maybe a little bit of both. Whatever it was, it was the first time I was conscious of the desire to be with one person so intensely. Johanna Kahn was the only woman who had ever made me feel this way. What was even more amazing to me was that it seemed she felt the same thing.

"Kissing you is amazing," she would say to me in the weeks following those moments that I wrote "Back to Sleep."

I wish I could remain in what is now like a collection of forgotten daguerreotypes. When we were together, it was as if nothing else around us existed—like it was the first time in history that it had ever happened. Once, we finished a bottle of wine and I put a candle in it. It became our official bottle that we would use as lighting every time she came over. The texture of her skin was lightly scented from a perfume whose name I never did discover.

I got to know Johanna's body in those first weeks. I remember seeing her two birthmarks for the first time. One was on her arm by her right bicep, the other was on her left thigh, just at the seam of her panties with a mini-bow at the front, which might as well have been a chastity belt, because of my VD.

I got to know her clothes too. She had a favorite sweater with stitching that was thick and holey which allowed me to peer through to her skin. Another outfit was a black dress with a red ascot—like the night at her party with Manu. If we weren't in a bar then we were in a rented ballet studio in Chelsea or the Upper West Side.

Once there was even a tango event by the center clock at Grand Central Station. She motioned to me to come over to her and attempted to show me some basic tango moves as people were racing to catch trains all around us.

"Hold me," she commanded as I placed my hand upon her waist, my other hand cupping her palm. Like I had told her the night we had our first date, I was much better at the hora and was now demonstrating that fact very well. We were surrounded by scores of people swaying back and forth like we were on the cobblestones of San Telmo, littered with cafes where people spilled out into the streets drinking wine. But we weren't in Argentina. We were at the hub for all points north of New York City where the rush hour foot shuffle surrounded us.

"Our teacher!" I suddenly heard from behind me.

I turned mid step with Johanna. Standing there were three women holding scores of pamphlets and waving directly at me like they were sending smoke signals to a plane in the sky, praying that it would come and get them off some desert island. It took me a second to realize it was three of my Jesus-Jew students doing their Jesus-Jew-pamphlet-handing-out operation, distributing leaflets with all the zeal of a new politician.

"Shalom! Yeshua surely works in mysterious ways," said Beatrice, wearing a flowered dress as usual. Priscilla was there too and she ran to me and gave me a big hug while I was still connected to Johanna. It was the warm embrace of a lost family member.

"Who are they?" Johanna mouthed silently.

A wave of panic came over me. What would she think? Thank God Gary Gangbang wasn't with them. He was probably too busy ordering tacos before the hooker showed up. After all, it was a Tuesday.

"He's our apostle. We love him," said Beatrice pushing Priscilla out of the way as she wedged herself between Johanna and me like a bubby *shepping nachas.*

"You take care of him now." She patted Johanna on the head, like she was handing me off to my new bride under the chuppah, "Yeshua has given you a blessing."

"Yeshua?" whispered Johanna.

"Don't worry about it," I replied.

"Bring your banjo on Saturday, our apostle!" said another one. The three of them waved in unison and walked off like they were three wise men who had just bestowed their gifts upon us.

Johanna stared at me and burst into the infectious laughter that

I loved. She laughed with her palms cupping her face and then threw her arms around me, her lips buried in my neck. I could hear the muffled sound of her voice. "Who are you, Mr. Check?"

"It's amazing that the whole charade didn't scare her away."

"You make a good point, Phil. If there was any moment that I expected her to run, it was that one. But instead, I could see that none of it mattered and that she was kind of falling for me. It had to be that. Why the hell else would she continue to consciously spend time with a banjo-playing-Jesus-Jew-Hebrew-teacher?"

Just as Johanna showed me her tango dancing and chocolate-and-cheese parties, I slowly plucked up the courage to show her my world as well. Once I took her to the monday night bluegrass jam at the Park Side Lounge, a Lower East Side honky-tonk that looked like it was a leftover set piece from the movie *Urban Cowboy.*

"What do you want to drink?"

"Do they have Prosecco?" she asked in all sincerity.

I pointed to the stage I was about to play on, a hand motion meant to say, "Probably not." It had streamers and strobe lighting on its perimeter. And everyone in the bar was drinking a shot of whiskey with a beer.

"How about a glass of red?" she asked, understanding my telepathy.

When her phone rang, she answered in French, apologizing to me. "I'll just be a moment."

Even the smallest snippet of dialogue that exited her lips always sounded like a line from a highbrow *Masterpiece Theater* mini-series. It was as if she had been born into royalty that she was unable to shed.

✿ ✿ ✿

For an entire month, Johanna consumed my thoughts and my time. And then suddenly, she was gone. She had left for Nairobi with Kofi Annan to monitor what apparently had become an African election crisis since the last time she mentioned it.

Her absence was a devouring madness that I didn't know how to process. I was left with all of these thoughts and feelings for her and fixated on all the vignettes of things we had done together in our super-short history. I wanted so badly for our relationship to continue to evolve while she was in Africa of all places. I received only one email from her in total: "Hey, Bello. I love it here. It beats New York."

I didn't hear from her again after that. It was radio silence. With no real information to go on, I was convinced she was now *shtupping* Kofi Annan. I imagined her black tango dress pulled up above her thighs on some hotel suite desk with her colorful ascot bouncing up and down on top of his international exoticness (probably with smegma too—*ugh, smegma*). I could almost feel the rhythm of her smacking her palms upon the wood to the lyrics of a song called "Secretary General," sec-thump, ra-thump, tary-thump, GEN-thump, ER-thump, AL-thump, sung by Kofi Annan himself with his quiet mystical voice and implacable accent as he *potched* her on the *tuchus*, his suit pants around his ankles exposing white tube socks with blue rings at the top. I was sure the other interns were resentfully recounting ballots in another room with all of the thumping sounds in the background, wishing they could have a piece of the action.

Whether she was banging the Secretary General of the UN or

was just too busy to answer my emails, a sadness came over me because I convinced myself from her silence that it was likely over. In my heart I felt that the real issue at hand, regardless of the fantastical trajectories of my imagination, was that if Johanna loved me, she would be communicative, even from Africa.

The void within me took over. A new melody suddenly emerged as I was strumming the banjo one night. I went to grab pen and paper and began to scribble some lyrics. It came out almost fully written. One of the lines went, "You put the hurt on me real good my darlin' / like a nail right through my shoe / maybe somehow there is some consolation for wanting what might not be you / after you pierced it through." I finished it even before Johanna touched down on the tarmac.

I dreaded seeing her the first time we were meant to get together upon her return. I could already hear her telling me it wasn't me, but rather her. We met downtown at Nolita House, a restaurant on the corner of Lafayette and Houston where I would come to play many bluegrass brunches with various bands over the years.

"I'm not feeling things," she said, just as I had predicted in my worst-case-scenario fantasies. "We should take it slowly and see where things go, maybe even be friends."

I really wanted to ask her why she felt that way and why she had decided to lay in my bed with me and kiss me for hours and hours if she just wanted to be friends. But instead, I just asked. "Are you sure?"

"Yes. And you are obviously looking for a girlfriend. I'm not ready to be in a relationship right now." Then she added, like she was firing me, "But I'd still love for you to be in my life."

The thought entered my mind that it must be the fact that I had VD, or that I was a Jewish banjo player or that I was a Zionist. And if it wasn't one of those reasons, then she had to be banging Kofi Annan.

"Are you sure you want to end things?" I asked once more, sounding more pitiful than I had counted on.

"Yes."

I went home and looked at the chorus of the song that I had already written. I was amazed at how prophetic it now seemed. "I could tell that you were already leaving, in the first kisses that you gave." I recorded it on my computer just like "Back to Sleep" with three-part-harmonies, banjo and guitar. And then out of spite, I sent it to Johanna that night, to let her know how I was feeling.

Later on she called me and asked, "Did you really write that?"

"Yes. I wrote it as you were flying home. I knew it was over, even before we met." I knew I seemed desperate, like a Norman Rockwell child hungry for an ice cream cone. But I didn't care.

"Matt."

For a brief second, I held out hope. Maybe the song had wielded some magical power to win over her affections again.

"Please don't write any more songs. It's unbecoming of you." The indifference in her voice stung. She was like Van Helsing using garlic to ward off vampires. It was obvious that she wanted me to back away and let her figure things out, whatever that meant. I concluded that I had been wrong about Johanna Kahn. Perhaps there had been a momentary flame of attraction on her part, but she had decided to blow it out with no explanation.

WANT TO MEET MATT CHECK IN THE FLESH?

Imagine traveling to a foreign country to be greeted by Matt Check. How about having him as your tour guide?

Want to make this a reality? Or maybe you just want to learn more. Use the QR code above to get information on how you can chill overseas with the author of this book.

https://www.parenthesespress.com/author-trips

CHAPTER SEVEN

On the Saturday following my breakup, I tried to look happy in class, but my Jesus-Jew students could tell that something was wrong.

"Why so forlorn, Matthew?" asked Priscilla.

"She ended things," I said to everyone as I put the chalk down, admitting defeat. "The girl I was tango dancing with in Grand Central Station," I clarified.

When they realized that they had met Johanna briefly, they all leapt up and came to console me, like we were best friends on the playground at recess.

"Don't worry, our apostle. We didn't like her!" Priscilla motioned with her girlfriend hand.

"Yeah, tango sucks," George chimed in, "it's not a real dance anyway!"

"Thanks, everyone." My messianic support system felt comforting, as strange as it was.

My students went back to their seats and I went back to finishing the phrase on the blackboard that I had been writing out. That day we had started working on the Biblical literary device known as the "infinitive absolute": when God uses the same verb twice, back-to-back in two different forms—that's when He means business. A famous example is when Adam and Eve are told in the garden *"Mot U'mat."* Both words are forms of the word "die" and it's a threat about the Tree of Knowledge. I was dissecting and explaining the construct of the second verb form when my cell phone buzzed. I looked down. It was a message from Johanna.

"Oh my Yeshua, she texted me!" I exclaimed. It had happened. Their strange way of talking had finally rubbed off on me.

The class leapt up a second time, rattling the desks and chairs as they charged to the front of the room, everyone elbowing each other in an attempt to see the message.

"What does it say?" Beatrice had jolted ahead of everyone in the pack.

"I wanna see!" Priscilla suddenly appeared underneath my left armpit.

I read the message slowly, like it was a note in a sacred fortune cookie, "I imagine your brown eyes engulfing me. I hope you are doing well, Bello."

"Oh, she DE-he-FINITELY misses you, Matthew." Beatrice patted me on the shoulder.

"It's so romantic," swooned George, his palm on his cheek. It was like I was suddenly in a parody of a Caravaggio painting, where I was Yeshua receiving some divine message on my cell phone and all of my disciples were standing around, impatiently waiting for how I would interpret this freshly sent bit of communication.

However, Priscilla had a completely different take on this new turn of events. "Cock-tease," she said, shocking everyone. She darted away from my armpit, returning to her seat quietly. We all stared at her as she calmly composed herself in her seat, her arms behind her head, ready to continue the lesson.

I was starting to realize it had been a mistake to let them know about my situation in the first place. "Everyone back to their seats!" There was a shocked silence as my students marched obediently back to their desks.

I had spoiled the mood of class. I tried to regain my composure. "Okay who wants to read the other examples on page 102?" I softened my tone, hoping to lighten the mood.

George raised his hand, "Oh, I can do that."

"How could she send you a message like that?" Beatrice blurted out from her seat.

"I know!" I threw my hands up.

"She misses him," George said, turning to the group. He was clearly the only one who had some successful love story to his credit. He kept seeing the positives, believing it would all work out. "It's all going to be okay."

"Tramp!" Priscilla shouted.

And with that, we forgot about the infinitive absolute for the day.

Johanna contacted me again a few nights later. "What's with the silent treatment? Surely we can be friends."

Why? What was the point of being friends? All of hers hated Jews anyway and loved smegma as the palate cleanser for Palestinian-Afro-Liechtenstein chocolate-and-cheese parties in Nolita, where only French was allowed to be spoken anyway. Johanna Kahn would never hear from me again. I decided right then that in her New York story, I would be the Hebrew grammar banjo boy from the subway with VD who came into her life to write a few songs about her only to vanish without a trace.

"And yet like a moth to a flame, Phil, I threw on my coat, left my apartment and tore down Broadway in an all-out sprint toward Avery Library at Columbia where I knew that she would be working."

"What happened to make you change your mind, Matt? Weren't you determined never to see her again?"

"There's no logic to what I did. It was like playing the banjo—I just knew that I had to do it."

I saw her sitting by the window typing away, probably about the history of the hijab. When she noticed I was there, she rushed to embrace me. For a second it seemed as if the odds were going to be in my favor. Maybe there was the possibility that we would reconcile our feelings, especially because she had reached out to me twice. But that's not what happened when we went outside to talk.

"You know that things will never work between us. I just want to be friends, really."

It didn't make any sense. She had made the effort to get in touch just to be friends? I wanted to understand her thought process. She really liked me, but she probably wished that I could be someone who would be more comfortable donning a keffiyeh and a Kalashnikov rather than a yarmulke and a banjo. "Is it because I'm a Zionist?"

She chuckled and was then silent. Maybe it was the warts.

"The VD?"

"Matt!" Her tone changed and now she was staring directly at me. "I want to be your friend! WE WON'T WORK OUT." She paused for a second, attempting to choose her words carefully.

And then she finally said it. "If only you could just let things be casual." It sounded like one of her classes in conflict resolution.

I felt like I was suddenly in a negotiation for feelings of mine that were being held hostage. And that word, "casual"—I always associated it with the idea of a 1970s European key party. It would have suited her. She was European and Europeans were into key parties and blurring the lines of friendship and intimacy. I just wanted to be her boyfriend, the classic American type.

She reached for my hand and attempted a smile. "I'm sorry, Matt."

"I'm in love with you and you want me to be casual?" I immediately sensed that I had gone too far. I knew the phrase was something I couldn't take back, though I had never said it before. Right away though, I understood the weight and feel of its grandiosity—like shooting a gun for the first time and feeling the recoil in my fingers, wrists, and arms. And though I had no experience with love, in that moment, I felt that I was in love with Johanna Kahn. But it didn't matter. She stared back at me in silence and I knew there was nothing more to be said.

Back at my apartment, I went to my bed and cried. It was a dry-heaving sob. It was the pathetic and loud bellow of a water buffalo that has just lost his mother to a band of tribal hunters and is now left to fend for himself, finding water all on his own and whatever it is that buffalos eat. How could Johanna want to move to a continent where water buffalos suffered so? And yet even as I lay there in frustration with her, every fiber of my being longed for her.

"I know what you mean, Matt. It was like the time that Nicole Kidman was supposed to have dinner with me at the Plaza and it all got spoiled because she decided to show up in jeans. I think she did it on purpose because she knew it would piss me off and that I'd cancel the whole thing right then and there."

"I'm not sure it's exactly the same thing Phil."

"But you see what I'm trying to get at, don't you?"

"Well...maybe? I don't wanna analyze your resentments around old flings. But what I will tell you about Johanna Kahn is that it seemed like she genuinely didn't want to be with me and so that's why I was confused that she had reached out again. The only rational explanation I could come up with was that she had spent the weekend in Marrakesh, with Sophie and Francesca, hanging out with Mustafa Ali of the Institut with no E at the casbah doing too many rails and ending up at his chateau in the wee hours of a north African morning only to discover that Mustafa wanted to give her 'The Salvador Dali'—and wasn't even kind enough to have a bottle of KY for the occasion! I mean who wouldn't want to go back to her banjo-playing Hebrew hipster after such an ordeal?"

"What does Salvador Dali have to do with any of this Matt?"

"I'm getting too far off topic, Phil. I've gotten to an important part of the story. This is where I write the song about Johanna with her name in it."

"That's how you're planning to end this chapter? That's your grand finale? Another song?"

"It wasn't just any song. It was THE song."

Another melody emerged that night. The idea that we weren't

meant to be resonated within me. It was the opposite of how I had felt when we met. She wasn't the first person in history to experience doubt about someone she had just met—but at that moment, that's exactly what it seemed like to me: "Joey you're not the last one / for sure you're not the first / girl in the world with these questions at hand / but questions ought to make us try a little harder / even if in the end, we're meant not to be."

I wrote the lines so quickly, singing each one out loud as I scratched the words into my notebook. The ink ran from the tears that fell onto the page. Perhaps overly dramatic and sappy, but true. I still have the pieces of paper in my memory box to this day.

I wrote a verse, a second one and then the final one. I recorded it on my computer with three-part harmonies, just like the other songs. I was in the middle of working on my new creation when I heard the buzzer. I went to the front door and pressed on the intercom. "Yes?"

"Bello? Are you there?"

I didn't answer right away. Was it really her?

"Kind of?" I heard myself joking. She laughed nervously on the other end.

That was when I understood that I wasn't supposed to ask about our status anymore. I could tell that she was struggling with forces I didn't quite get. But she was still giving in. By being with me, she was leaping off some cliff and just going for it, whatever it was.

"Buzz me in."

In the apartment, she whisked herself into my bedroom and dropped her backpack to the floor without saying a word. She collapsed on the bed next to my banjo. Then she saw the pages of paper on my blanket and the fresh ink.

"Please tell me you didn't write another song."

"Just wait until you hear it."

I picked the banjo up and gave it a quick tuning. The expression on her face seemed to say, "Really? You have to play the banjo right now?"

But this changed when I began to sing the words of our story thus far. Maybe she understood it as little as I did. I certainly wasn't the one who would have been able to explain it to her.

Regardless of how the song characterized things, having her there and playing it for her was nothing less than a mystical experience for me. And it achieved the effect on her that I had hoped for—it won her over.

"Make love to me." She pulled me to her and began to take off my shirt without even asking.

And I said the first thing that came to mind. "What about my VD?"

"Bello, you are so annoying."

"And that was the first time that Johanna and I made love, Phil."

"And what is it you most remember about that night?"

"She told me that I was the first circumcised man she had ever been with, yet another time that a woman noticed the Semitic nature of my member. Instead of counting sheep, I was now counting Nazis with foreskin. Ugh, smegma."

CHAPTER EIGHT

Finally, Johanna and I were in stride and it seemed that we were actually in agreement that we were having a relationship. It felt like we were spending every Friday night together. If we weren't at Epistrophy then we were at another local wine bar in her neighborhood. And afterwards I was always invited home. On Saturday mornings we got brunch with mimosas. It was always at Public, Johanna's favorite spot, just up the way on Elizabeth, north of Spring Street.

Things were finally good between us. We were settling into a comfortable routine. However, the day I knew that she was genuinely taking us seriously happened because she asked me to buy her toilet paper. I had just gotten off the subway and was on my way to her place. "Charmin Ultra Soft with the little bear on the front," she said over the phone.

"Really?" I was shocked that I now knew one of her more intimate secrets: the type of TP that she used to wipe her European *tuchus* with.

If my new role as purchaser of her bathroom products wasn't enough of a confirmation that we were an item, any doubts of mine were removed when she suggested that we should consider traveling together. We never made any definitive plans. Instead it became a sort of extended game. We'd go back and forth about different potential destinations.

"If we traveled, where would you take me, Bello?"

"Why don't we go to Madrid for a week?" Other than Aruba and Israel, it was the only place that I had been and it seemed the type of location that would impress her. "I'll show you my favorite neighborhoods and cafes. We can drink wine and listen to jazz." I only hoped we wouldn't bump into La Reina de la Stank.

But of course she'd already been to Spain a million times and would explain that she was thinking of someplace a little more "exotic." "How about Turkmenistan?"

And then I would counter with something like, "Turkey? Yeah, how about Turkey? It sounds like Turkmenistan but is probably only half as dangerous."

"How about Kenya? Nairobi is so beautiful. We could go on a safari."

A safari actually sounded doable until she'd add something like, "And while we're there, we can visit the tribe in the northeast part of the country, who rarely resort to cannibalism at all as long as you speak a few grunts of their language."

African countries were her favorite. But even better was when the place didn't have a written language and the natives communicated amongst themselves with clicks, grunts and sneezes. Johanna often made me feel like I was a senior citizen who liked to take cruises with midnight all-you-can-eat buffets, compared to the places that she wanted to go.

"What if we stuck to this hemisphere—like Aruba?" I could stomach one happy island. I imagined us at Playa Linda overlooking the beach. Plus, compared to other Caribbean nations, there was probably no Japanese encephalitis.

"No way. Aruba is way too boring. How about the Amazon?"

"But where would we shower?"

"In the river, silly."

I imagined bathing in the river and having a *candiru*—the microscopic vampire fish—swim up inside my penis and start breeding other little baby vampire fishes before expanding my *shmeckel* into the shape of an amoeba. "Joey, couldn't we think about places where there aren't deadly diseases?"

"Oh, don't worry, Bello. We'll get all the necessary vaccinations first. And malaria isn't anything to worry about. It's just an extended high fever."

Even though I couldn't imagine taking a vacation to any of the places she suggested, the very fact that she wanted me to come along meant that she was taking us seriously in the real world. If I was at Johanna's side, maybe I'd be able to stomach Nigeria or Siberia or Transnistria. Whatever type of ailment I got would run its course.

For the first time in my life, I felt like I was in a real relationship. "My girlfriend," I said probably a bit too often for my friends' tastes at school. I would tell them how her hair was such a mess when I woke up next to her on Monday, or I'd chuckle when I recalled out loud how she almost spilled the coffee over breakfast on Sunday. I loved being with her, I loved talking to her and I loved talking about her.

Yes, things were going just great. In fact, everything was going better than I could ever possibly have hoped for.

And that was when we saw *Paradise Lost*, an acclaimed film from the mid-aughts about two marginalized Palestinian mechanics from Nablus with nothing to lose, so they become suicide bombers.

The screening was being hosted at Columbia's School of International and Public Affairs. And it happened to be facilitated by none other than Manu.

"Nazi horse dung smegma boy?"

"Yes, Phil."

Though Manu was no longer a romantic threat, he was still one of Johanna's buddies that I had to see on occasion. When the film was over, Manu stood before the audience, facilitating a Q&A with the sincerity of a French revolutionary as he talked about symbolism and metaphor, backed up by facts, figures and fluency about the Palestinian political and social situation.

"Manu really loves the Palestinians," I whispered, attempting to be funny. "It's like his porn."

"He loves them because Palestine is a beautiful country and it deserves to be free."

It was the first time I suspected that the differences in our political views might actually become an issue. I had been to the Palestinian territories, to Ramallah where Johanna claimed it was pretty in the spring and where Manu had visited the *Mukataa* that he pronounced so beautifully with his guttural Arabic *qoph*. I had visited this mythical Palestinian capital of the self-governed West

Bank in 2005, at a strangely quiet time in the history of the Holy Land's conflict. It was just a few months after Yasser Arafat's death and a few months before the disengagement from Gaza. It was a year-and-a-half before the Second Lebanon War. It was two years before Hamas was elected to run the Gaza Strip, and just shy of two decades before the events of October 7, 2023.

When I was there at least, Ramallah had seemed like a quiet and pretty city. Its flattop stone architecture reminded me of other old cities in Israel proper like Haifa, Acre and the Nachlaot section of Jerusalem, except that everything in Ramallah was in Arabic. I knew that I was a ten-minute drive from Israelis but I felt like I was in a foreign country. The only thing that reminded me that we were remotely near the Jewish State was the currency, the shekels that I used to buy dinner at an Italian restaurant near the center square. (I ordered a calzone of all things—it was surprisingly good.)

I had arrived and left through the military checkpoint at the Qalandia refugee camp, with nineteen or twenty Israeli soldiers brandishing guns that were bigger than they were. In crossing over from either side there was lots of trash, barbed wire, lines of people and even a row of turnstiles which to me was the most absurd and humiliating part of all, because I associated them with baseball stadiums, not contested political territories that contributed to the hardship of the entire Palestinian population. From the whole experience, I suddenly understood that this land was more complicated than I had been told about in my childhood Jewish education. After that day I still felt that Hebrew was the eternal language of Israel and the Jewish people. But I was a changed person forever too. I believed the Jewish settlers and the military should leave the occupied West Bank and Gaza once and for all, allowing the

Palestinians to finally have their own sovereign nation state.

Even though I thought I was open minded, the political leanings of Johanna and her friends were different from mine. There was this attitude that even though peace needed to be negotiated, Israel shouldn't have existed in the first place—like it was an uncle with a coke habit who we didn't speak to unless we needed something.

That word: Palestine. When Johanna said it, it sounded so provocative to me. Even after my experience in Ramallah, it was still an uneasy word for me to use. It was much easier to say Palestinian Territories, the West Bank or to call the people that lived in those areas simply Palestinians. But to refer to the land as Palestine seemed far-fetched. There was no official Palestine, at least not since the partition of 1948.

If only I could have put her political perspective into the same category of things I didn't really want to encounter but knew I would, things like leaving used tissues on the nightstand, having morning breath and the eventual chancing upon a match floating in the toilet bowl freshly filled with new water. Those were the kinds of personal details I dreaded learning about, but knew I could get over. Politics fell into a different category though. It was not as simple as discovering that my girlfriend had bodily functions like everyone else. The rights of the Palestinian people—this was a more serious matter.

"Honestly, Phil, I would have preferred learning that Johanna Kahn liked getting the 'Salvador Dali' after a golden shower and few potches in the tuchus rather than have to attempt to reconcile her feelings about the Jewish state and my love of Hebrew."

"I feel you, Matt. Right after Claire and I divorced I was dating a Hari Krishna."

"It was as if I stood for everything that she was against."

"Yeah, if her weirdo chanting with cymbals hadn't interrupted my strength training exercises in the mornings, it might have worked out, but that's life, I guess."

I didn't realize how much our differences were bothering me until I ran into someone from my past, someone who was pretty much the opposite of Johanna. I was in a café working on a paper about the revival of the Hebrew language by the Zionist pioneers in the early 20th century. I was reading one of the chapters from a seminal book about the subject, Benjamin Harshav's *Language in Time of Revolution.*

When I went to refill my coffee mug, I passed a table with a woman I definitely recognized from somewhere. We made eye contact and I could tell that she too was trying to figure out how we knew each other. Then it suddenly came to me. It was Maya, the woman from that night on the mountaintop in Israel I had met a few years beforehand.

"Maya?" I asked, making my way toward her. It was hard to believe it was really her.

I could tell she was still trying to place me, so I reminded her. "We sang together a few years ago in that village Ein Hod."

It took her a second to process what I was saying. "Oh my god, you're right! You played the ukulele!"

"The banjo."

I joined her at her table for a few minutes. I told her about my life in New York, my studies in graduate school and my aspirations of being a Hebrew teacher. She patted my head, like a nephew, just like the last time we had seen each other. The action brought back the beach, the wine, the cigarettes and the night we met. Even so, I couldn't bring myself to imagine anything happening between us. There wasn't even a hint of flirtation from my side because I was so consumed by my relationship with Johanna.

"You're still a *matoki*," she told me, patting me on the head a second time.

We both burst into laughter, as if it were some private joke of ours, which it was. It was like looking at an old photograph from a different time and being amused by how much had changed.

She rummaged through her bag and retrieved a business card. "Give me a call sometime. Maybe we can play music before I leave for my next tour."

On the card was a picture of her wearing a thin, white and transparent veil. Her eyes were dark and mysterious. Her name was spelled out in papyrus font, as if she were the daughter of some Levantine king. Her job title was simply "singer."

"It's really great that you love teaching Hebrew," she told me just before we said goodbye. It was such a simple sentence, but in hearing it, I realized that these were the words I'd been longing to hear from Johanna.

☆ ☆ ☆

A fresh round of fighting broke out in Israel that season, which I suspected was not going to be good for my relationship. Johanna's Facebook status let all of her friends know that she was beyond horrified. "Israel, do you have no limits, no shame, and no humanity?"

Manu was the first to respond to her posting. I could practically hear him moaning over the keyboard, typing his thoughts vigorously like he was stroking himself, fantasizing about saving Palestinians in the same way that Gary Gangbang thought about prostitutes, high fives and tacos on Tuesday nights. "I think we can all agree that bombing a tiny, overpopulated piece of land with F16s is a tactic to terrorize."

The smegmatist's diatribes were followed by a similar vein of opinions from the rest of Johanna's chocolate-and-cheese bohemian cohorts. All of it nagged at me, like the sound of a dripping faucet on the one night that you happen to be starved of sleep— you try to ignore it, even though you're dying to leap out of bed and scream at the inanimate object to shut up as if it were actually going to apologize for keeping you awake. But I decided to ignore it, knowing there was a bigger picture to consider. After all, I wanted the love I felt I had fought for to last. And this meant that I was not going to mention either Facebook or the Israeli-Palestinian Conflict the next time I saw Johanna. If we could simply talk about other things, we'd be fine. So that was my plan.

It was an evening that began as they always did with us, with a glass of wine and a little kissing on her couch. We talked about our respective weeks, me with my Hebrew, banjoing and Jesus Jews and her with the world's crises to study and solve. She mentioned her briefs on Kenya and a new project she had been working on: an ongoing negotiation with some FARC shoot-off revolutionary group in the jungles of Colombia, which she was excited about.

"I'd better brush up on my Spanish because I might even get to go," she said, making me think that what she actually ought to do was bring the extra two-ply Charmin Ultra that I had bought her, just in case the FARC prison cell toilets didn't have any toilet paper when she was captured.

Met with my silence, she changed the subject. "Bello, did you see the pictures of the tango party that I just posted?"

It was as if she knew I was trying to be on my best political behavior, but I refused to be drawn into her Palestinian web. I would be a good Israeli and not be tempted to respond in a disproportionate manner from a couple of Katyusha rockets that were somehow innocently lobbed into my territory. "Where would I see your pictures?"

"On Facebook, silly."

"Nope, haven't been on lately to be honest." I had seen them. I had studied them actually, looking for signs of anti-Zionism in every tango gesture. But I refused to talk about it.

"Oh, you HAVE to see this new spot on the Upper East Side," she said, opening up her Facebook page and handing me her laptop. "You'll just love it!" What I really would have *loved* was to not look at her page with her. Then all the comments from the Israel-bashing-session-complete-with-tango-dancing would not be right in my face.

"Joey, I'm not really in the mood to look at Facebook."

"Oh come, come. Just one second." She leaned over her laptop and began typing.

"No, thanks." I took the laptop from her, closed it and put it down on her coffee table. I began to kiss her neck, reclining her onto the couch. "Let's look at pictures later."

She pushed me away abruptly. "What's wrong with you?"

"Nothing."

Now she was suspicious. "Something's definitely up." There was a pause. "Just tell me, Bello. Tell me how you feel."

I took a sip of my wine and put it back down on the table, "Okay," I sighed. "How could you write that?"

"Write what?"

"Oh you know, Ms. 'Israel, have you no shame?'"

At first she didn't understand. "What are you talking about?"

"The political comments between you and your friends on Facebook."

She suddenly understood that I was talking about the war in Gaza. "It was a healthy and open conversation about our views."

"Really? How are the things that you said healthy?"

"You know, you're right. I don't want to talk about this."

"But now we are."

"You can be so ridiculous sometimes, Matt."

I was suddenly angry. "You know what's ridiculous, Joey? The fact that if this were Poland in 1942, you and your kosher vagina would be in the same fucking transport to Bergen-Belsen with the rest of us! There, I told you how I feel."

We both stared downward, sitting next to each other for a few minutes as if we were in couples therapy, but there was no analyst sitting across from us and there would be no closure to the conversation either. I wanted to defend myself and the things I stood for. I also wanted to salvage this *whatever-it-was* I was going through with the supposed woman of my dreams. I said the first thing that came to mind. "Now let's look at your pictures."

But she didn't look up from the table. I could tell that she too was wrestling with too many conflicting thoughts.

I took one more sip of my wine and stood up quietly. "I'd better go."

I hoped she would stop me, but instead she walked me to the door. Neither of us said a word as she let me out. There was only the sound of the latch and key.

✿ ✿ ✿

Johanna and I were not in contact for two whole days. This was the longest we'd gone without talking since the week of silence when she was in Kenya not banging Kofi Annan. For me it was maddening. I tried to go about my business with my studies, my lessons for my students and practicing the banjo, but instead I found myself checking my cell phone at every opportunity.

I finally broke down on the third day. I was downtown and on my way to the Park Side Lounge for the jam. Johanna knew I would be there since I went every Monday. "Hey, I'm in the neighborhood. Would love to stop by." It was a simple text, but it said everything. If she wasn't going to break the silence, then I would.

My phone buzzed just as I was entering the bar. I expected it to be her, but it was Dad. He was the last person I wanted to talk to. I didn't want to check in unless I had good news. Still, if I didn't pick up, I knew I'd never hear the end of it.

"Hi, Dad." I tried to sound enthusiastic, which was not the way I was feeling.

"Who's this?"

"What do you mean, 'Who's this?' You called me!"

"Oh, right. Well, who is this?"

"Your son."

"Oh, my son. Which one?"

"Matthew."

"I don't have a son named Matthew." He was being sarcastic. He thought this was hysterical.

"Dad, I can't really talk now. I'm about to start…"

"Hold on, I'm gonna put you on speakerphone with Mommy so we can have a threesome. Hey, Gail! Your baby's on the phone!"

Click. "Hi, Matt."

"Hi, Mom."

Before Mom could say anything else, Dad monopolized the conversation again. "So when are you finally gonna get the subway girl off the subway?"

"Don't rush him, Ronnie!" I could always count on Mom to come to my defense.

I wanted to tell them that Johanna was coming home eventually to meet them, but I suspected this wasn't true. She would rather be in some mythical country that was a combination of Nairobi and Ramallah—the Palestinian Congo where Ebola babies wear keffiyehs and brandish AK-47s.

"I'll only scare her a little bit, don't worry," Dad insisted. "And if she's too skinny, we'll fatten her up with pasta."

"Dad!"

"What? I'm just saying…You've been talking about her for two months already. I wanna meet this girl from the subway even if she's British!"

"I gotta go, guys. Love you both."

I hung up and ordered a Pabst and a shot of Jameson. I finished the round and ordered another, and an extra shot of whiskey. I was going to get drunk.

Seated at the bar. I thought about the three songs I had written for Johanna. She knew all the words to "Back to Sleep" and "Pierce it Through" and of course, to the song with her name, "Joey": "Questions ought to make us try a little harder / even if in the end we're meant not to be."

I felt the buzz of my phone and with it came a surge of hope. This time the text actually was from her. But it wasn't the message I'd been longing for. "Hope you have a good jam, Bello. It's probably not the best night for you to come by. Let's talk tomorrow. xxx"

"You're always pensive and drinking whiskey every time I see you," said a woman sitting next to me.

She looked familiar, but I couldn't quite place her. She was about my age and dressed in jeans and a flannel. There was a hint of an older era about her, one of picket fences, Southern porches and mason jars. It was the length of her hair. It belonged on a farm with horses and country music. I liked that.

"Where have I seen you before? Do you play?"

"I just like music. I come to a lot of the jams."

"What's your name?"

"Jane Pines."

"Pines is a famous last name."

"Oh, yeah? Whose?"

"An early Zionist thinker named Yechiel Michel Pines." I went on to tell her that there was a street named after him in the storied Tel Aviv suburb of Neve Tzedek and that I loved that neighborhood. I found myself talking about the year that I lived in Israel and how I used to go to Neve Tzedek specifically to walk around its windy streets at night.

"It was an early cultural enclave of Jews living in Palestine in the early 20th century," I explained, as I suddenly imagined myself and Johanna living in the second Aliya with our pioneer spirit, draining the swamps, building a new society in Tel Hai, Rosh Pinah and Zikhron Ya'akov right alongside David Ben-Gurion, Golda Meir and Berl Katznelson. (I imagined that Golda was really good at swamp draining. Not so much Beryl.) I would have been a school-teacher in the first Hebrew kindergarten, and I would have looked like Paul Newman the entire time, writing the *alefbet* on the chalkboard with a Sten gun strapped to me. Johanna would have been teaching in a kindergarten as well, with the Palestinians of course (not that there would be anything wrong with that).

And everything would have been fine until the Jaffa riots of 1921 when Arabs killed one of the legendary Hebrew writers of the Second Aliyah, Yosef Haim Brenner. I would have gone to his shiva with David and Beryl and Golda, expecting to introduce all of them to Johanna when she would show up to meet me there, at least in time for the egg salad and lox. But as I waited and waited, she'd never show. In fact, she would turn out to be the first woman in Palestinian history to be waving a flag in disapproval of the Zionist movement in the streets of Neve Tzedek—and right on Pines Street too! "Is your girlfriend often this late?" Golda would ask and I wouldn't have any idea how to respond. I'd just take another silent bite out of my egg salad sandwich.

And that was when I saw things between Johanna and me for what they really were. Johanna wasn't going to celebrate the things that I was passionate about. In fact, she was going to be critical of them for the rest of our days together. I needed to see her immediately and break things off.

I paid my bill and put my banjo on my back, ready to leave.

"Where are you going? You haven't even played one song." Jane, this stranger in front of me, sounded disappointed that I was leaving.

"I have some unfinished business to take care of." I didn't care if I was being abrupt or even slightly hurtful. I didn't owe her anything. I needed to see Johanna. With the banjo on my back, I tore east on Houston Street towards Nolita. I was at her apartment only ten minutes later.

She answered the buzzer with surprise. "Hello?"

"It's me. I need to talk to you right now. It's important."

I climbed the steps to her apartment and the door was already open. The way she looked at me made me think of a foreign language professor in college taking off her reading spectacles, biting on the ends while pondering the content of her plebian student's needs.

I was out of breath like a dog in the summertime. The alcohol of the final beer and shot had already gone to my head. I really didn't know what message I wanted to deliver now that I had arrived but it somehow involved a peace agreement between Arabs and Jews once and for all.

"You're drunk, Matt."

"I need to tell you something."

"It couldn't wait until we made actual plans?"

"No."

I was facing the bathroom. I could see the toilet and the Charmin Ultra Soft package with the smiling bear on the front. There were two rolls left. I thought about her wiping her European *tuchus* with toilet paper bought with my money. And somehow that was what came out of my mouth.

"I'm taking the toilet paper."

"What?" I could tell she had no idea what I was talking about.

"You heard me."

Morning. Sunlight. Throbbing head pain. I came to on my couch. On my coffee table I spotted an empty bottle of Rioja, four empty bottles of Stella and the two rolls of Charmin Ultra. My ashtray was full of half-smoked cigarettes, my pack of Parliament Lights totally empty. Tortilla chips were strewn all over and crusted salsa too. The only thing missing was a collection of used condoms on the floor. I tried to recall if I took a cab or the subway home but there was no memory of anything. I rubbed my temples with the fingers of each hand, suddenly embarrassed at how the night had ended. I would need to apologize. I could only hope that Johanna would agree to at least get together for a bite to eat or something so I could attempt to explain myself. I checked my cell phone. There were no texts or calls, neither outgoing nor incoming. It meant that we hadn't been in contact after I left.

I made a pot of coffee and sat down in front of my laptop readying myself to write an apology to her. I tapped on the keyboard and after entering my password to my email account, I was immediately aware of a highlighted new message in my inbox. It was an email from *Royal Air Maroc* thanking me for purchasing a ticket on a flight scheduled to leave that night from JFK to Casablanca.

"What the fuck?" I whispered to myself.

Maybe it was some type of spam that made it into my inbox. After all, I had googled Morocco at some point while dating Johanna. But when I clicked on the link, I was suddenly seized with terror as I looked at the official confirmation number for my flight and my seating assignment too. Had I really bought a plane ticket to Morocco?

I racked my brain. The last thing I could recall was the echo of Johanna's voice in the hallway, calling after me like I was a bandit in the night as I descended the rickety stairs of her apartment building. But buying a plane ticket? It was totally absent from my memory.

"I can't go to Morocco," I said out loud to myself. It hadn't even been twenty-four hours so surely I could get my money back.

But when I looked at the details, I realized that the ticket wasn't refundable because I had bought it through a third-party website, not to mention that the flight was scheduled to leave that evening. That's why it was impressively cheap for such a long flight. It was under $1,000 round trip and non-stop. I had even gotten an aisle seat (my favorite). That was pretty cool.

"Morocco, huh?" I said to myself, as if trying on a new shirt. It sounded nice and exotic. "Morocco!"

And then for some reason, I just decided that I was going to take the trip. Not to mention that it might prove something to Johanna once and for all. I too could go to Africa and take part in some amalgamation of tango, French, and chocolate and cheese, even with my American accent.

Still hungover, I cleaned and did laundry. I called my bank and credit card company and let them know that I'd be out of the country. I packed a bag and stopped at Barnes & Noble for a *Lonely Planet* guidebook on my way to the airport. In the terminal while waiting for the flight, I called my parents, letting them know that I loved them and where I was going.

"What did your father say, Matt?"

"Don't go, son! Your bowels!"

CHAPTER NINE

The day I arrived in Marrakesh, I wandered the streets of the medina in the desert heat, continuously amazed that my undergarments could be soaked all day long. If I contracted dysentery, there would be nothing to come out because I was so dehydrated. I think I finally understood the Biblical story of Jonah and why he had asked God to kill him when the Almighty took his shade away. It must have been a Moroccan heat—the dry-heaving, energy-depleting, beads-down-your-ass-crack kind of hot. (Gary Gangbang would not fare well in a place like this with so much stink. He would definitely need to invest in ventilation—though on the bright side, every meeting would be ethnic night because he, his sex buddies and the prostitute on call could have all the couscous in the world.)

I hated the heat. I hated the stink. I hated the way that the heat made *me* stink. But more than that, I just hated being alone. I was bored and lonely sitting in a coffee shop facing the famous *Jemaa el-Fnaa* square in the center of town, where I smoked cigarettes, drank coffee and watched soccer matches on an old rusty television. My solitude was coupled by the frustrating realization that I was alone in another continent and it was all my own doing.

When the muezzin sounded the call to prayer at dusk, the voice over the loudspeakers was like an air-raid siren, blaring the phrase in Arabic, "Allahu Akbar!" (God is great), just like I remembered from my time in the old city of Jerusalem. Then a sea of men would flood into the streets, running for their various places of worship, some to shops, some to larger mosques that I passed along the way. Those trying to walk in the opposite direction of foot traffic, caught in the torrent, must have felt like salmon trying to swim upstream in the high tide of a Muslim river.

I was so bored and lonely in Marrakesh that I began spending great quantities of time with the only English-language piece of literature that I had brought with me. In fact, soon I was not only re-reading Ernest Hemingway's *A Moveable Feast* but was also translating it into Hebrew, because there was nothing else to do. There were two possible words in Hebrew that I could think of for the word "feast." One was *S'udah,* the modern word used for "meal" (which I thought appropriate because it shared the same root with restaurant). But then there was the biblical word for "feast," *mishteh* (which has the same root as the verb for "drinking"). In the book of Esther, *mishteh* is the word used for the famous Bacchanalia of the Persian King Achashverosh. He got so drunk that he asked his wife Vashti (whose name also shares the same root for the verb for drinking) to dance for him and his friends. And when she refused, he had her killed. Yep, that's the kind of story that Hemingway would have enjoyed: drinking, chauvinism and a touch of violence.

I attempted to interact with the locals on my second day, hoping that going shopping would distract me from the heat.

"Hey you!" a man yelled at me. "I got what you want right here!" He motioned for me to enter his shop.

"*La, shukran.*"

"My friend! Please!" He was suddenly at my side, shaking my hand with both of his. "My name is Hassan. You are most welcome to my store!" He wore a charcoal suit, with an open collar and no tie, along with a fez and a mustache. I took my hand back and was about to continue on my way, fascinated by the fact that Hassan was putting so much energy into getting me to buy a rug.

"*Habibi, la shukran.* I'm not interested in buying any rugs."

"Where are you from?"

"New York."

"My friend, you cannot get a rug like this in New York. Please?"

"How much?" I felt like I was in the scene from *Life of Brian,* being convinced to argue for a goat mask while running away from the Romans.

"Because I have cousins in New York, I'll give you a special price. $300!" He flicked his wrist in an upward circular motion like he was a magician revealing a hidden jack of diamonds.

I knew that I had made a mistake even talking to this guy. But I couldn't just walk away now. "You want me to give you 300 American dollars for one of those?" I pointed at the two large carpets hanging from the ceiling.

"How dare you!" I had suddenly angered him.

"You are not a good man!" he shouted after me. If he had had a scarf, this would have been the moment when he would have draped it across his shoulder and traipsed away from me. All I could do was shake my head.

I went right back to my hostel where I was happy to once again be alone in a country I felt so incapable of understanding. I wished I had stayed in New York after breaking up with Johanna. I wished that my drunken decision had been to take a trip to the Jersey Shore because the boardwalk pimps that I had encountered during my summers visiting my Bubby and Zayda outside the Tropicana were nothing compared to these Moroccan rug dealers.

In an internet café I wrote an email to my parents, lying about how much fun I was having:

Hello Mudda, Hello Fadda,

I am here at Camp Morraka! I'm alive! After landing in Casablanca, I took a train to Marrakesh. Yes, just like the song, but don't worry, Dad, I didn't smoke any hash. This city is so great. I'm having a wonderful time walking around, smelling the spices in the market, wandering the streets, eating couscous and meeting some very interesting locals. The people are so willing to talk to strangers and the prices are great. Say, if you need a rug, I can get you one for $300. Hope all is well back home.

Love you—Me

P.S. (for Dad) I promise not to drink the water. I remember

your story about a business partner of yours and the parasite he contracted in Moscow after accidentally drinking from the hotel room faucet one morning when he was hungover. Yes, Dad, only bottled water for me.

After pressing send, I checked my inbox. There was some spam and a few emails from professors about end-of-the-semester assignments. There was one message from school about a cocktail reception for us graduating students, which I quickly RSVP'd for. There was an email about the next jam at the Park Side lounge that I would miss by just a day.

And there was an email from Joey. So she decided to write to me. I had texted her from the airport just before the cabin door was closing. Maybe it was immature, but I couldn't go all the way to Africa without Johanna knowing about it, even if it was an obvious attempt to prove to her that I could be as interesting and daring as she and her friends were. My text had been very simple: "I'm on my way to Morocco." It must have confused her that it was the one and only communication between us both since I had left her apartment with the toilet paper. And now in Morocco, I was receiving her response:

Bello,

Seriously? You've really outdone yourself this time. Are you really in Morocco? Who are you? I've been calling and your phone is still off. Will you please just give some sign of life? I hope you're not just doing Jewish things. ☺ Joke.

If you are really there, I hope you are having a good time. I'm so jealous! It's hot in the city right now and just reminds me of Kenya. Oh, I miss Africa. Why didn't you invite me? Perhaps we could have sorted things out while away from this crazy city.

Well in any case and whatever happens, if you make it to Marrakesh you might as well visit Mustafa Ali since you're there. I've copied you on an email to him. It's in French, so you won't understand it but he'll be expecting you if you go to the institute. Can we please talk when you get home?

Bisou xxx,
JK

"Oh, Mustafa again!"
"Yes, Phil."
"The guy from the French Institut of Marrakesh with no E, what Joey had whispered into your ear clandestinely on the first night you spent to-gether at Epistrophy. The sex addict, ball-gagging, white snake-snorting dude who was tag-teaming Johanna and her friends with the se-cre-ta-ry gen-er-al after their long night at the casbah?"
"Correct."

Johanna's email roused my spirits. Visiting Mustafa Ali was an opportunity for me to show her once and for all that I *could have been* the man of her dreams and have her eternally frustrated with this fact too. Yes, she would be forced to see that I could be like Manu, Francesca, Sophie and Sophie's androgynous zebra-striped boyfriend who talked about *films*. I could be bohemian and go meet random strangers, eat couscous, talk about interesting subjects while interspersing a couple of words in Arabic and French and come home with some great stories about far-flung regions of the universe that are meant only for conversations in downtown wine bars. The cherry on top of the experience would be if Mustafa invited me to the casbah. That's where we would do a couple of rails off the clavicles of his mistresses while he simultaneously gives me a history lesson about Morocco as a constitutional monarchy with every bump. I couldn't wait to meet him.

His address was in the new part of Marrakesh, seated in a valley with palm trees like it was a desert oasis, a tranquil respite from the noise of the ancient market. When I found the institute, it was like discovering some emerald city. It was a large compound with expansive walls and an iron gate at the front. There was a young lady at the reception desk wearing a polka dot silk ascot.

"Mustafa, *s'il vous plaît*," I requested.

"*Bibliothèque*." She pointed to a staircase behind me immediately, as if I had said some secret password.

Up the staircase and through a glass door was a quiet library with stacks and stacks of books. At a desk was a young man with perfectly combed and shiny black hair that reminded me of Omar Sharif.

"Hi, I'm looking for Mustafa Ali."

"I am Mustafa."

I looked at him for a second, processing the fact that this was *the* Mustafa Ali at the French Institut of Marrakesh with no E, the same man that Johanna had mentioned on our very first date. There was nothing *disco* about him at all. Nothing exuded anything that had to do with drugs or strange sex positions. He was as calm as if having just finished a yoga class. I already imagined him walking up to the Peace and Mediation Smoothie Counter and ordering a small kale and blueberry slushy in baggy tan pants recently bought on a trip to Hampi.

"I'm a friend of Johanna Kahn."

"Oh, you're the friend she mentioned might visit. How is she?"

"Oh, she's good," I said with as much enthusiasm as I could muster while thinking that she loved the Palestinian Congo more than she could ever possibly love me.

"Are you in the same program?"

"Not exactly," which was an understatement if ever I'd made one.

"What do you study?"

"The Tanakh. It's kind of like..."

"Ah, the Hebrew Bible."

I was astonished. I thought I had heard him incorrectly. "What?"

"Isn't that one of the words you use for the Bible? The Tanakh?"

"Um, yeah."

"I have a book in Hebrew at my house that I bought in Paris. I have no idea what any of it says though."

And that was how Mustafa invited me over for a meal the next day to meet his wife and two sons. He lived just down the street from the library above a shopping center.

The apartment turned out to be small and sparse. It wasn't much larger than my place in Manhattan, yet it housed an entire family. Clara, Mustafa's Belgian wife, answered the door with a smile and brought me into the living room. Their two sons were in highchairs, both toddlers with dark curly hair and inquisitive eyes. Mustafa put his hands on both their heads and rustled their hair with his fingers playfully. "This is Qais and Isa."

"What do their names mean?" I asked, expecting him to tell me his sons had been named for family members who had passed.

"Qais is my favorite pre-Islamic poet and Isa is my favorite Arabic scholar." He was obviously proud of this. "Come, let me show you my books."

We walked over to his bookshelf where he had books in Arabic, French and English. There were classic novels, scholarly journals and volumes of poetry.

"So tell me what this book is." Mustafa took out the lone tome of Hebrew that he had mentioned back at the library. It was a *Mikraot Gedolot* (the Great Sources). I had just coincidentally taken a course on the rabbinic literary genre known as *parshanut* where I had read week after week from a volume similar to the one he was holding. Now I was thousands of miles from Manhattan, in some random person's house, looking at the very same text and being asked to explain it.

"This is not technically a Tanakh. It's just the Torah, the first five books of the Tanakh. But look. Let me show you what's cool about this particular volume." I leafed through it and pointed to all of the margins. "These are rabbis from different eras in history, interpreting the text, verse by verse."

"I see." He was fascinated. His fingers passed over the lines of the sagely exegetical art of Ibn Ezra, Abarbanel and Kli Yakar.

"This guy is the Rashbam. He's the grandson of this guy over here named Rashi. They were both medieval rabbis."

"Is Maimonides here? He wrote in Arabic, right?"

"Yes, he did." I was amazed at the depth of his knowledge. "He's not here though."

We sat down at the table and Mustafa began feeding little Isa baby food. As he passed me a plate of carrots he told me that he wanted to learn Hebrew one day.

"Why's that?"

"Because it is related to Arabic and therefore I guess your people and mine are related too."

More than anything, he longed for a time when Jews and Mus-lims in the Arab world could coexist and understand each other more. For him it all began with language. He loved poetic and lyrical Arabic verse, both modern and ancient. That's why he named his children after his favorite writers. He had this theory that he would love Hebrew just as much as Arabic if he only could read it. He thought both languages and cultures would ultimately be able to understand each other through their literary sensibilities. I sud-denly felt as if I had stepped into a chapter of Kahlil Gibran's *The Prophet*. Had I just discovered a Moroccan version of myself?

For the first time in my life, I could see Johanna and me mov-ing to Marrakesh. To Africa of all places! On Saturdays, Mustafa, Clara and the boys would come to the apartment that Johanna and I had rented in the medina. We would continue the philosophical discussions that we had just begun. I would even give Mustafa some Hebrew lessons. And eventually we would work for peace together. And if Johanna and I had a son we too would name him Isa, or maybe the Biblical version: Essau.

I finally understood that I had ended up in Morocco for a rea-son. I had gone halfway around the world to meet a man she'd mentioned casually on our first date and as a result, Mustafa from the French Institut without an E had led me to believe that maybe Johanna and I could make it work after all.

Two days later I found myself in a synagogue on Erev Shabbat. One of the prayers was being passed around from person to person and everyone in the room took a turn reading a line. When I found the spot to follow along, I was fascinated by the accent. I was able to make out the words being uttered, but the Moroccan accent for

Hebrew was almost incomprehensible to me.

When it was my turn to read, I was amazed that no one ac-knowledged my own accent. We were reading from the "Song of Songs," a biblical story about two young lovers who pine for each other. We were at the part when the woman in the story proclaims, "Here comes my lover, leaping over mountains," as if her groom was a gazelle on the desert dunes of the biblical wilderness of the Aravah Desert.

Transported by the story, I was pulled into my own fantasy:

I am under a Moroccan chuppah, along with all the old men in the room, some of whom have just signed my ketubah, standing around as witnesses. My parents are at my side looking rested and relaxed because they have just spent the afternoon lounging at a pool with Johanna's parents at the Club Med back in the heart of the medina, even though Ron Check is complaining that every meal was served in a tagine.

And then there is my bride, all in white, radiant and just about to be mine. I take a sip of wine from the *kiddush* cup. Her white veil is lifted and she takes a drink. Afterwards, she circles around me seven times. Finally, I place the ring on her finger, uttering the sacred and timeless phrase, "And thus you are betrothed to me." She smiles, only the two of us knowing that our own little Isa (or Essau as we were going to pronounce and spell it) is already growing inside of her, that we will be feeding him baby food in less than a year's time.

It is perfect. It is beautiful.

CHAPTER TEN

I was in a taxi back to my apartment when I called Johanna. My airplane had just touched down and I hadn't even dropped off my backpack at my place. I knew that there was a chance that she'd just be getting off work or would be finishing up at Avery Library but I couldn't wait to speak to her. While I was expecting her to say, "Let's just see each other after you're rested up," to my pleasant surprise, she suggested that we get drinks. Maybe meeting Mustafa and the imagined wedding in a Moroccan synagogue were in fact the cosmic signs I had been waiting for all along.

We met at a wine bar on 95th and Broadway. She was dressed in one of her business outfits, black pants and a cream blouse, and had a warmth about her that was kind of surprising.

She grabbed my hand while listening intently to me, sometimes rubbing or patting my arm. She seemed relieved that I made it home and that we were with each other. Whatever she was thinking, I would take it. I felt triumphant as I recounted the stories of my time away: the Moroccan rug salesman, my meanderings of the bazaars around Jeema el-Fnaa, the call to prayer from the muezzin, dinner with Mustafa and the experience in the synagogue.

"I told you not to do Jewish things!" she said as the check arrived.

"I know, I know...I couldn't help myself."

"And I can't believe you met Mustafa. That's incredible."

"Excuse me." A voice called to us from an adjacent table. It was an unassuming man in his forties drinking alone. He had a flamboyant accent.

"Yes?" I said.

"I just wanted to say that the both of you sound like the most interesting couple and you look great too!"

"Really?" I asked.

"Yes! You're so rugged, and your girlfriend, or whatever she is, is super *Euro-cosmo*. If you're not gonna have kids, I hope you have a lot of Yorkies and Schnauzers instead!"

"My girlfriend?" I laughed looking at her.

"Well, I guess I am."

In my imagination, I had already planned our wedding (or at least the Moroccan version of it). But this was the real thing. Getting Johanna to admit that she was actually my girlfriend was the real-life equivalent of the Moroccan chuppah. I couldn't believe the words that had just come out of her mouth. After months of emotional ups and downs, I had finally arrived at the seemingly triumphant "well I guess I am." It was like finally winning that little stuffed unicorn at a roadside truck stop diner claw machine, after hopelessly going through years and years of pocket change in tired desperation.

✿ ✿ ✿

My birthday was coming up in a few days and I couldn't wait to celebrate with Johanna. There was just one small problem.

"Is this the part of the story where you couldn't get it up while trying to whack off one morning?"

"Phil, when did I ever give you the impression that I had erectile dysfunction?"

"I could have sworn that when you first solicited me that it was part of our convo."

"Not from my side of things Phil. I was probably just telling you how much I laughed at the opening pages of The Counterlife.*"*

"Really? I could have sworn you said something about a traumatic experience around this time that involved a weird porn about Torquemada you happened to see in Times Square."

The small problem was this: I had returned from Morocco with a violent stomach bug that decided to make its presence known two days after returning to New York. This stomachache wasn't just any old infection. It was a violent wringing of my intestines, the kind I had never before experienced in my life, one that produced a black-and-watery stool that I had only read about in books.

"It's just like the time that Maureen shat herself in My Life as a Man!*"*

"You see Phil! That's why I wanted you to be part of my story."

"It's my birthday in a few days!" I texted Johanna from the toilet one morning. "That's great, Bello! Don't make plans. I want to surprise you!" she wrote back.

We continued to text back and forth with frequency during my days-long convalescence. Maybe, just maybe, I could look forward to seeing her on my birthday and if I wasn't feeling a hundred percent, perhaps she'd just bring me some chicken soup and we could hang out for a few minutes before I'd need to send her home (so she wouldn't have to hear me in the bathroom).

I woke up on the morning of June 16th to many messages from friends and family. There was a great voicemail from my father. "Bum! You're twenty-seven. Stop going to school and GET A JOB. Call your father when you wake up. Happy birthday. I love you... usually."

My brother left me a voicemail, calling me an old bastard and my Aunt Robbie and Uncle Jacob from Texas left me a recorded message of them singing "Feliz Cumpleaños" as they had done every year for as long as I can remember. But all this was overshadowed by the fact that as morning turned to noon and then noon to afternoon, the only person that I had not heard from all day in the barrage of texts, emails and phone calls from friends and family, was Johanna Kahn. She was radio silent, even as the day turned into late afternoon. I was confused. She had said that she was my girlfriend, had said, "Let's do something fun for your birthday," and here I was again, back to where things always seemed to end up with us.

I was angry and anxious and suddenly needed to get drunk. I didn't care if there was a risk of me having an accident of my bowels opening up in the bar. I had been cooped up for days and I needed to get Johanna off my mind. There were plenty of dive bars on Broadway that weren't that far from home. I picked the first one I saw, saddled up to the bar and ordered a beer and a shot of whiskey. Then I ordered another round. It was a hot Monday in June. The Mets were on the television. It made me think of the episode in *Saved by the Bell* when Zach claims to be Jewish to get out of school on Rosh Hashanah only to be seen on television at a Dodgers game.

"Let me buy you another round. You're drinking as quickly as me." The man on the barstool next to me was in his early thirties, wearing a Mets baseball hat. He had a can of Pabst in front of him. We clinked dram glasses and took a shot together.

"What's your excuse for day drinking?" I asked.

"My wife left me."

"Oh, I'm sorry to hear that." I was genuinely concerned. Yet at the same time, there was something comforting in hearing about someone else's hardships in light of my own. Maybe his situation was similar to mine. Maybe I wasn't the only one in the world trying to make it work with a half Heb Brit who'd rather be monitoring elections in Baku and shtupping foreign dignitaries than working on a relationship she was in denial about being in.

"I'm not. I'm relieved. I'm happy I didn't have to do it myself!"

After that there was nothing else to say. The wisdom I was hoping to get from this encounter never arrived. We sat quietly drinking side by side. I might as well have been alone. I was left to the silence of my thoughts about Johanna. With every subsequent sip, the more resentful I felt.

I was quite drunk and at peak resentment by the time the rumblings of my stomachache returned. Judging by the sound and motion of the churning, I knew that I had just about ten minutes until the floodgates would reopen.

"I gotta go." I said out loud to no one really and slapped a twenty-dollar bill on the bar.

I tore down Broadway almost in an all-out sprint, knowing that I didn't have very long until I'd be soiling myself in public. Every half block, I had to stop and clench my butt cheeks for ten seconds, while my intestines knotted up inside me, like some imaginary force was wringing me like a rag just for fun.

I got to the lobby of my building with beads of sweat on my face. I jabbed at the ancient black-and-circular elevator button over and over again like I was playing a game at the arcade, waiting for it to arrive, hearing the beep of it passing floor after floor which felt like an eternity. The whole ride up my legs were crossed and I was breathing rhythmically as if I was doing some sort of strange yoga pose.

Inside my apartment I didn't have time to take my wallet and phone from my pants. I dashed for the bathroom and barely had my pants down to my ankles just as I heard the ding of a text on my phone. On the toilet, I pulled it out and there it was, the message from Johanna that I had been waiting for all day. "Happy Birthday Bello! What are we doing to celebrate? Just let me know. I'm easy."

I'm easy.

I'll never forget how I felt about those words from the toilet. I remember staring at them with every spurt that came forth. The resentment I had felt in the bar had turned to simply sadness. Nothing was more genuine than her actions, or lack thereof. I really just needed to end things with her once-and-for-all. And so that's what I did. I broke up with Johanna Kahn over text from the toilet, drunk and pissing out my ass.

"Actually, Joey, we're finished."

"What?"

"Yeah."

"You can't be serious?"

I never responded. I just stared at our final exchange, like I was watching the image of her disappear in the rearview mirror as I drove away.

"I've been there, Matt."

"You mean you've broken up with a woman over text while drunk and on the toilet?"

"Oh no, I'm not that kind of guy and I never really figured out how to text well anyway. My version of break-up was literary in my day—a long letter in the mail detailing all the ways that it would and could never work out (and reviewed by my analyst of course)."

"And what would your reasons be?"

"You're too close with your children. You don't take walks with me. You don't like sex enough. You're still resentful about the prenup. Your sweaters are too crunchy. I told you that a nondisclosure agreement means you can't write a memoir about me."

My bowels were empty and at peace for the moment, though I was still drunk from all the beer and whiskey. The ceiling spun while I lay in bed, attempting to keep the text exchange on my phone in focus, as if it were a sacred artifice that had preserved something very special to me. I fell asleep at some point, though it was the kind of half-slumber with a weightiness to it that didn't allow me to really slip into true rest.

At dawn, a single thought shocked me back into awareness. I shot up straight in bed. I burrowed my face into my pillow and screamed as loud as I could for five seconds.

"AHHHHHHHH!"

My head emerged, like it was the end of one of those demolition machines that breaks up concrete. In a way it was. I had initiated the destruction of something that I seemingly loved very much, but also something with a faulty foundation that never would have lasted in the long term. And so I had reduced it to a pile of rubble from the seat of my toilet the night before.

I dove my head back into the pillow for a second round of screams.

"AHHHHHHHH!"

This time when my head came up I was crying. I said the syllables in Johanna's name, stretching out the sound of each vowel, hoping to make the sound last longer.

"Joooo-haaaaan-aaaaa. Jooooo-eeeeey." Suddenly I imagined her downtown in her bed in Nolita, holding a glass of red wine with a smirk on her face, totally relieved that she was rid of me. Yes, she was free and excited about what her next party would bring with guests like Manu or Kofi or Mustafa or whichever subsequent Nazi-Palestinian-smegma-producing non-Jewish Banjo playing anti-Zionist she could find.

"I LOVED YOU!" I shouted at the top of my lungs, "LOVED... YOU, YOU FUCKING BITCH!"

I collapsed back into bed continuing to clutch my pillow in a fetal position and continued to whisper, "I loved you. LOVED YOU."

CHAPTER ELEVEN

The six months following my breakup with Johanna are not a time in my life that I like to recall. I felt that I had lost something valuable and irreplaceable and that nothing would ever matter again.

The first few weeks were characterized by a drunken blur at the same bar where I had met the guy going through a divorce. Day after day, I drank alone to oblivion. I'd stumble home, fall asleep and barely wake up in time for my classes.

As weeks became months, eventually I cut down on my drinking. As miserable as I was, I got tired of living in a cycle of perpetual blackout-and-hangover. There was still a dark cloud over everything I did, but I tried to move forward anyway, albeit in slow motion. It was not the time in my life when I had the luxury of standing still. I had recently graduated with my master's and it was time to get on with my life.

Instead of having a positive attitude towards landing a job as an amazing Tanakh teacher (which is what I had wanted to do all along), I felt mostly the need to prove to my father that my year in New York was not a fool's errand. I was seized with anxiety at the thought that there was no more delaying "the real world." Perhaps my anxiety would have been quelled had I gone through at least one successful interview at any of the multiple Jewish day schools where I had applied. All of them either rejected me or didn't get back to me. My dream of becoming a cool Hebrew teacher, waxing philosophical with budding intellectual kids looking to me for nuggets of wisdom about the minutiae of Hebrew grammar—it just was not happening so easily.

"So how did your father actually take all of this?"

"He called me a bum and added, 'Goddamn bubble mower.'"

"The bum part I get. But what's with the bubble mower?"

"It's a toy my mom bought me when I was two years old. At the time my Dad was sure it was going to ruin my life. I would waddle back and forth across the living room, wearing my OshKosh overalls with a protruding diaper, spewing bubbles around the family room like it was my own private county fair, filled with a happiness richer and fuller than any other I had experienced thus far in life. However, Ron Check was not pleased. No son of his would be predisposed to a future as a landscaper, one of the professions forbidden in my life's intended trajectory. 'Take it back to Toys "R" Us right away! Why would you want to encourage a thing like that?' he shouted to my mother. Now, he seemed to take some pleasure in having proved his earlier prediction right."

My father's attitude every time I'd call to check in about my job search made it seem like I was currently on the verge of weeding poison ivy in the balconies of rich Park Avenue apartments.

"God damn bubble mower," he mumbled again at the start of our next phone call.

"Oh, stop being dramatic, Ronnie," my mother said, attempting to keep the peace. "Matt, we know that you're trying."

"Yeah, trying to MOW LAWNS!"

"Roooonnnnnnie!"

After months of failing to get a job, I only had one option left. One of my fellow classmates told me that the synagogue where she worked part time was looking for a new principal to be in charge of its Hebrew school. She thought I would be perfect for the position and put in a good word for me with the head of the search committee.

The last thing I wanted was to work in a synagogue. When I thought of synagogue education, I imagined the senior rabbi's Bible & Bagels class every third Thursday in the Sarah and Bernard Livschitz Family Library, full of retirees complaining about the awful urn coffee with the faint combined scent of old tuna fish and crusting egg salad, followed by the collective after-meal gastrointestinal chorus coming from the senior citizens. I didn't think that a synagogue education was legitimate. Plus, it seemed smelly.

Though it was not the future I wanted, neither was moving home to deflect knives from my father. On the day of my interview, I walked into the main building of the temple in a traffic-choked high-rise construction enclave of Manhattan. It seemed like the last place in the world that a synagogue should exist. But right there on an unassuming corner stood the building in all its European architectural glory, built a century earlier when the neighborhood was still populated by horsedrawn buggies.

As soon as the interview began, I realized that I had not considered at all the type of job I had applied for, nor had I done the necessary research. The executive director, a professional yet friendly woman named Judith, explained that this was a large and storied congregation. They had programs for all ages, from toddlers to seniors and I would be in charge of a lot. While it sounded interesting and like a great opportunity, I knew I was in way over my head.

What did I know about running a school? I was twenty-seven and had never had a real job aside from teaching Hebrew to Jesus Jews, which apparently was the only population I would ever teach Hebrew to—or at least it seemed that was what the universe was trying to tell me. But it was too late to escape.

Judith brought me into a conference room to meet with the search committee members, all dressed in business attire and seated around a long wooden rectangular conference table where one lonely and empty seat in the center was reserved for me. It was as if I had just been picked up by the Soviet NKVD and was now going on record to sell out my comrades in the resistance.

"You're fresh out of graduate school with no management experience," said a balding man in a suit. "You'll be in charge of a staff of teachers pretty much the same age as you. Will you feel comfortable in such a position?"

Well, I had been a unit head at a camp for a summer, but I had been awful at it. All I remembered from that summer was the time that we got stuck on the Brooklyn-Queens Expressway and I had to help little Teddy pee into a Snapple bottle because he couldn't hold it in.

Still, I managed to turn this memory into a job-worthy answer: "I was in charge of five counselors in summer camp where I spearheaded fun and educational activities that allowed the kids to grow and socialize, all the while infused with Jewish learning."

The balding man nodded. I could tell I had scored points for using the word "infuse." It was an overly used term in all of my education seminars.

"What's an example of a moment when you were outside your comfort zone as an educator and succeeded?" asked a woman in a gray suit.

My time with the Jesus Jews sprang to mind. However, this probably wasn't the place to mention that I had taught Messianics how to read Hebrew. Luckily another example came to mind: Haifa. I mentioned working with marginalized grade school Arab kids in Wadi Nisnas and how through teaching them to play chess and soccer, "They came to know a Jew without a gun." The committee melted as I told them the story of how little Ibrahim called me his father ("Moti, Atah Abba sheli") on my last day of my volunteering experience.

"Johanna would have been proud that you used the term margin-alized."

"Thanks, Phil."

Too bad for the committee that they didn't ask enough of the right questions. I knew nothing about management, discipline or administration. I didn't even know how to use Microsoft Excel (which they also never asked me about). It seemed ridiculous that I was being taken so seriously. When I walked out of the interview, part of me even hoped that I wouldn't get the job because I knew I wasn't qualified. It was obvious and they would figure it out once they all compared notes and looked at the other resumes in their pile. After all, they were professionals from profit-making enterprises. I was certain they saw right through me. My time in New

York was up. I was ready to raise my white flag, pack up my boxes and move home. I had made a valiant effort.

Judith called me a few days later. "Matt, we'd like to offer you the position."

I was completely stunned. "Really?" was all I could think to say.

"Yes, really." We both laughed.

"Amazing! Can we talk about salary and benefits?" I had been prepped by a guidance counselor to "Never say yes to the first offer, no matter how much someone offers you. Always negotiate." Whatever salary she offered me, I was supposed to say that I would get back to her and think about it.

"Yes, of course. How about starting with $67,000 a year and full benefits."

I had to cover the mouthpiece of my phone for a second to process the amount of money I had just been offered. There was no need to negotiate. As far as I was concerned, I was rich!

"Okay, that's good for me," I said, trying not to sound too excited.

"Wonderful! Mazel tov, Matt. We're excited to have you aboard. I'll email you a contract this afternoon."

"And what about your father, Matt? What was his reaction?"

"He screamed."

"AHHHHHHHHH! YOU DID IT, MATTHEW! Hey Gail, he got the job! And he's making $150,000 a year too! He's practically making what a lawyer makes!"

"Dad I'm not making…"

Click. "Congratulations, honey!"

"What are you calling him 'honey' for? He's *my* son! And he's a principal too! Good job, Mr. Kotter! I'm proud of you, son—*my* son!"

"Thanks, Dad."

"Now turn in my credit card. Apply for your own!"

☆ ☆ ☆

When I landed the job, the first thing I thought of was my Je-sus-Jew students. They had known that I was looking for full-time work that whole spring and told me they had prayed for me, want-ing me to find the best thing out there. It was as if the prayers that they said when they ate the wafers along to the sounds of Hatikvah had actually been answered.

Only Priscilla seemed bitter, but that was to be expected.

"Why are you going?" she asked jealously, as if I had found a new lover and was packing my bag to steal away in the night. "Did you find a better place to teach Hebrew, our apostle?"

"No. I've just gotten a full-time job."

"You think that you can just leave us?"

"You should be happy for him! He's been looking for work for months! Let the man tell us where he got a job, Priscilla!" George was standing as he said this, the rest of the students hushed by his outburst.

Looking at everyone, I suddenly got sentimental. I realized that I was going to genuinely miss them. We had come so far together. Now I was like Kevin Costner at the end of *Dances with Wolves*. I was one of them and I understood them too, even though I came from a totally different reality.

"I'm going to be the principal of a Hebrew school."

"My prayers have been answered! Thank you, Yeshua!" shout-ed Beatrice in a full out sprint towards me. She threw her arms around me and squeezed me tight until I couldn't breathe. She was more excited about me getting the job than I was.

"We're proud of you, our apostle!" George said, patting me on the back.

The rest of the class followed suit, coming up to hug me and congratulate me—even Priscilla. It was in that moment that I understood that my experience of being *Matthew the apostle* had been an important part of my life. I never thought that it would be a little sad when it finally came to an end—but it was.

My first day of work was anticlimactic. I didn't get to meet any of the students or teachers I'd be managing since school had already finished for the season (everyone would return just after Labor Day). I could tell, however, by the way that all the staff talked about the chaos of disciplining privileged Manhattan children that I had started my tenure in a "calm-before-the-storm" period. It was clear that once September arrived, we'd all be very busy.

I was grateful that things weren't too hectic right away. There was nothing interesting or glamorous about the work I was doing in those first months. I had never really worked in an office before and there was a steep learning curve for me with all of the "onboarding" (a term I had never heard before). I had to learn how to use the database, company email and Microsoft Excel. Before that year I had never heard of the term CC or BCC (I had always just put everyone in the "to" column of my emails) and I didn't even realize that you could copy and paste text (I had always just retyped everything).

The biggest drama that I had to deal with was not even at work—it was taking the subway. Having lived and gone to school uptown, I had been shielded by the chaos of rush hour. It was especially awful in the summer heat, when everyone was waiting on the platform longing for their train to arrive, sweating in the heat with buttery skin. Once the train finally showed up, there was this push and shove into the car as if we were all attempting to flee oncoming zombies.

Almost every morning, the train would stall underground without warning or explanation. People would elicit groans and sighs while looking at their watches—everyone was always seemingly late. My prize after emerging from the belly of the city and heading to one of the coffee kiosks was a cheap donut and cup of weak coffee in a blue Chinese plastic cup.

As strange as commuting was to me in those early days of my first real job, neither the subway nor the trials and tribulations of learning Microsoft Excel could hold a candle to what turned out to be the strangest and most challenging aspect of my job as a Jewish educator: Tot Shabbat.

"Tot Sh'what?"

"You know Shabbat services—but for tots."

"You mean for babies?"

"Yep."

"Do you want to know why I never had kids, Matt?"

"Tell me, Phil."

"Because eventually, years down the line, I knew that I'd have to pay for yet another person's therapy in addition to my wife's."

What did I know about educating kids that young at that point in my life? The thought of spending Saturday mornings in a room full of screaming, diapered toddlers while nursing a hangover and smelling of Lower East Side bars didn't seem appealing. And to make things worse, I had a song-leading partner whose name—"Miss Julie"—made me think of an old cat lady living in a rent-controlled apartment on 1st Avenue with decades-old unvacuumed Persian rugs and a cat litter box in a stained bathtub.

However, when I showed up the first time, Miss Julie was nothing like the cat lady I had expected. She was attractive and around my age, with long blond hair parted down the center like a folk singer from the early seventies.

"You're Miss Julie?"

"Ugh, I hate when everyone calls me that. It makes me sound like a bag lady."

"I know. I was thinking the same thing!"

We laughed. She shared my sense of humor at least.

"So you're stuck here on Saturday mornings too?"

"Yep. The families love it though. It's actually not that bad. You'll see."

But it was that bad. Miss Julie took out her guitar and began to play the first song for me before the children arrived: "A Dinosaur for Shabbat." It was far worse than I could ever have imagined. The lyrics involved inviting a dinosaur to a shabbat dinner. She was obviously desensitized to the fact that she was singing about a violent and extinct prehistoric carnivore coming to the dinner table to dine with children (and not on them) on the holiest day of the week.

"This is a real song?" I asked, once she finished playing.

"Ha ha, yep. Why don't you be Pierre today when we sing it? She reached into a plastic bin containing child-friendly objects like tambourines and shaky eggs until she pulled out a stuffed red hand-puppet dinosaur with a kerchief and a beret. "Zeees eeez Pierre," she said with a French accent as she made the puppet lean backwards dramatically.

I was still trying to process the idea of American dinosaurs at Shabbat. Now they were going to be French?

"MISS JULIE! AHHHHH!!" screamed the first of the kids to enter the room, running toward my new song-leading partner with glee and sticky fingers.

"Hey guys!" She welcomed them with open arms and hugs.

The room quickly swelled to at least thirty people, half of them screaming toddlers. The other half of the population was adult, amazing me at how happy a person could be at 9 a.m. on a Saturday morning.

"I have a new friend today who's going to be joining us on a very special instrument called the banjo. Can we all say banjo?"

"BANJO!"

"Okay, kids," Miss Julie said with a warm and sunshine-filled voice, "who's ready for Shabbat?!"

We warmed up with two more ridiculous sounding songs: "Chicken Soup for Shabbat" and "I've got that Shabbat Feeling." And then, as if to prove that my entire life had added up to one huge zero (or rather one purple French dinosaur), we arrived at the moment I had been dreading. Miss Julie knocked on her guitar as if to mimic someone at the front door: "Who could it be?"

"A di-no-soooo," said little Todd pointing with one hand, while the other was stuck in the back of his pants, scratching his butt.

"A giraffe?" asked Miss Julie playfully.

"A di-no—soorrrr!" shouted Anna, who was a little older and

able to pronounce her letters better.

Miss Julie looked at me to get Pierre ready. It was time to bring him out with his little prehistoric eyes and his hat and majestic ascot. I wanted to strangle the little French fuck!

"Oh, a dinosaur!" exclaimed Miss Julie.

"A DI-NO-SAUR!" yelled all the children once more like The Beatles had just walked onto the stage of *Ed Sullivan*.

"Why, *bonjour*, Pierre," added Miss Julie.

Everyone in the room was now quiet and fixated on my hand, waiting for me to answer. By that point in my life I had been through things that tested my resolve and had survived them: trials that ranged from being treated for genital warts to successfully getting into and out of Palestinian areas of the West Bank all by myself. But at that moment, on that morning, with parents and children staring at my hand, waiting for it to speak, I realized that I had never been so afraid in my life. And then I spoke in my best French accent.

"Well, *comment allez-vous* zjjjulliee…"

Laughter could be heard from the crowd. I felt a twinge of triumph. I could do this. It wasn't that bad.

"So how is Shabbat going for you this weekend, Pierre?"

"It eeezzz *tres bon*," I said with the accent of the chef from *The Little Mermaid* as if singing the song "Le Poissons". Everyone laughed again. I figured that after my two comments, I should do what dinosaurs do, make a loud roaring sound.

"So Pierre," asked Miss Julie, "Why don't we sing your favorite…"

"RAWRRR!!!" I was starting to get into this.

"Your favorite song, Pierre."

"RAWRRRR! RAWRRRR!" I finally got the hang of it. The kids simply loved the dinosaur. I put him in a little girl's face and let out another roar.

At first it was just her screaming, but the sound proved to be contagious. The boy next to her screamed and then broke down in tears. Another child began to cry and then a third from the back of the room. It was suddenly a tidal wave, a wall of sound that could be heard out on the street. They all cried into the breasts of their perfectly dressed cookie-cutter parents because I had apparently shown them the dark side of a puppet.

"Ha ha humph. Oh, sorry."

"Are you laughing at me, Phil?"

"Oh, not at all. Just the image. You, a master's, a banjo, and a room full of terrified babies. And all your dreams completely crushed. How could I laugh at that?"

BIBLE + BAGELS CLASS
EVERY THIRD THURSDAY
IN THE SARAH AND BERNARD
LIVSCHITZ FAMILY LIBRARY

CHAPTER TWELVE

The same month that I became a Hebrew school principal I moved into an old factory loft space in the hipster enclave of Williamsburg, Brooklyn with two roommates, one of whom was my brother. I was hoping to hold onto the bohemian-musician side of my personality, counteracting my "jobby-job" in Manhattan and also staving off whatever effects that Tot Shabbat and the purple stuffed dinosaur were having on me.

Our loft-apartment was so big that I hosted bluegrass "pickin" parties that whole summer with all the people I had met at jams during my time in graduate school. We'd climb out my window onto the roof of the adjacent building and play all of our favorite songs with the Manhattan skyline in the background.

There was a part of me that felt like this was my version of participating in an artsy circle of my own like Gertrude Stein's

Parisian Lost Generation, writing their 20th-century postmodernist prose, or Allen Ginsburg's West Village Beat scene and its spoken-word poetry, or even the Haight Street hippies in the sixties starting their sexual revolution along to the psychedelic sounds at the Fillmore West.

There was never anyone special, but always someone interesting. Like me, they were all in their twenties with jobs, living in the Big Apple and attempting to make some sense of the adulthood we were still trying on for size.

One Friday night I put my banjo down to take a break and struck up a conversation with a girl wearing black eyeliner with black hair with a bowl haircut. She looked like Winona Ryder's character in *Beetlejuice*.

"What's your name?" I asked.

"Xandra—with an exclamation point."

My initial thought was that this was a name that could only be said with hand gestures by George on *Seinfeld* —Xandra!

"What kind of a name is that?"

"I made it up."

Conversation and music came to a stop when my brother appeared at the front of the room wearing his white chef's apron. He was in culinary school and had cooked an entire meal that evening for everyone that had come to the party as practice for one of his classes.

"Spotty was born to Link and Hilary, on a farm in upstate New York." Tonight Jon was telling our guests the life history of the cow now on our plates. "He grew up in a totally non-abusive and grass-fed environment. One time Spotty escaped and crossed the creek to the other side. He was the adventurous type. Any questions?"

The room was silent and staring at him.

"Well bon appétit and l'chaim people!" There was applause and people raced to the buffet to dish up Jon's elaborately prepared meal.

Later that night, after Jon and I had cleaned up, I was about to get ready for bed since I needed to get up for Tot Shabbat in the morning, but saw Xandra! in the living room. She was seated with the few remaining guests watching TV in Spanish. Our television had a makeshift antenna made from a recycled dumpster coil we'd found in the alley and the only channel we got was Telemundo.

"So Xandra! Wanna have some whiskey in my room?" I said after approaching her.

She seemed not the least bit surprised at my question, as if she'd been expecting me to eventually come around.

Xandra! followed me into my room. My banjo and attempted translation of *A Moveable Feast* from my trip to Morocco were lying next to each other like a cat-and-dog odd couple on the blue divan.

I poured us two glasses of Jameson, clinked a toast and sipped. We sat on my bed looking out the window together at the Williamsburg Bridge and lower Manhattan in the skyline just across the river, as if staring at a landscape painting on the wall.

For a little while we made small talk about the dinner, the music, about the neighborhood and about voting for Obama that fall. I thought we were both circling around the very reason she had left the couch watching TV to join me: to hook up. Since breaking things off with Johanna, I didn't want a relationship or even to date casually. But I was open to having some fun if I hit it off with someone. If a hook-up occurred with Xandra! because she was intrigued by my banjo and my apartment, then good for me.

She moved closer to me which I interpreted as her giving me the sign that I was supposed to make a move. But I wanted to be a little bit drunker first.

"One more?" I asked.

"Sure!" she said without skipping a beat.

After both of us had downed a shot, we took another and then another and yes, then another too. After that, we started kissing immediately, like we were actors and someone off screen had just said to us, "Kiss! Now!"

It was raw, sloppy and desperate. I don't know what was going through her mind even though she was acting exactly like me, but for me it was like scratching an itch that I hadn't been able to get to for a long time. I was horny. I wanted to feel a woman's naked body next to mine. I walked us over to my bed, like we were in some type of a summer-camp relay race where we weren't allowed to be detached from each other. We fell on the bed simultaneously, and began to take our clothes off while we laughed and breathed heavily.

The last thing I remember is us in our underwear and kissing before I blacked out. All of a sudden, I was alone and it was morning. I had no recollection of how things ended with the girl whose name included an exclamation mark.

"Fuck," I said out loud.

I had to be in Manhattan in an hour for Tot Shabbat.

My body hobbled like it usually did when I was hungover. I waded through a Red Sea of the previous night's left-over bottles and cigarette-filled ashtrays. On the other side of the living room was the bathroom where I would sober up and become presentable before confronting Pierre and the screaming children.

As I expelled the previous night's farm-to-table sensibility, as the water in the shower poured over me, as I brushed my teeth, as I shaved, suited up and shouldered my banjo to leave for Manhattan, I felt a deep sense of emptiness. I didn't want a girlfriend. I wasn't ready. But I also didn't want a string of anonymous one-night stands I barely remembered the next morning. The problem was that there really wasn't anyone for me to call for even the possibility of a hookup. And then I remembered Maya.

"Who?"

"You know, the Israeli singer I met in Ein Hod, who I bumped into at the coffee shop in Morningside Heights while reading Benjamin Harshav's seminal work, Language in Time of Revolution, *during the waning days of my courtship with Johanna?"*

"Oh, that Maya. Got it. That Harshav book sounds like a riveting read by the way."

"I can send the Amazon link, Phil."

Maya and I were friends on Facebook but I hadn't thought of her much since running into her at the coffee shop. I had been too consumed with Johanna. And she had a boyfriend anyway, at least that was what she had told me back in Israel, in the wee hours of the morning when she dropped me off at the gates of the *moshav* and drove off into the sunrise.

Still, a lot of time had passed since then. Maybe her situation had changed? I decided to text her like it was no big deal.

Me: Hey, it's Matt. How've you been? I'm having a party tonight. Wanna come? It'll be fun.

Her: Hey, I'm good. Maybe. Send me the details in case I can make it.

Me: Very cool. Hope to see you soon and that all is well.

✿ ✿ ✿

That night, Jon served up another one of his culinary school recipes to a crowd of talkative and hungry hipsters. This time the cow's name was Gustavo, which for some reason made me think of beef tacos.

As more people showed up to the party, as the music got louder, I continued to gaze longingly at the front door, but it was always someone else arriving, never Maya. I got more and more annoyed as the night went on. She had only responded "maybe" to my message but that "maybe" had given me hope. She didn't owe me anything. So why was I feeling like a jilted lover?

She was an international type, not unlike Johanna. The thought occurred to me that she probably had some Scottish guy for a fling (it seemed like Israeli women in the diaspora always had Anglo boyfriends). She probably considered herself worldly and exotic because she was dating some dude with a leather jacket that had red pubes and ate Haggis. His name was surely Angus or Malcolm, or maybe Bram or Duncan (like the band Duncan Sheik that I had always hated).

Later on during dinner that night, I cleared the empty entree plates off the table with a surprising amount of resentment given that this woman really meant nothing to me. In the kitchen, I angrily let the dishes crash into our porcelain industrial sink to hose them off, just as Jon came in to plate the dessert.

"Dude! What's wrong?"

"Nothing." I began scrubbing. Jon knew I was hoping that Maya would be there.

"There are so many girls here. It doesn't matter, man."

That was easy for him to say. He had a girlfriend.

"Forget Maya and forget Xandra! Go talk to someone bro. Go make it happen!"

I approached the first girl I saw. "Oh, is that a Nepali necklace? It really suits you. Hi, I'm Matt Check and I live here."

The stock hipsterette with lipstick and yet-another-bowl-haircut-parted-like-a-sea-down-the-middle-of-her-brow-roots responded perfectly. "No, I wish. I bought it at the Salvation Army up by Spike Hill. Isn't it fuuuun?"

"Totally."

I hated when places, food and clothing were referred to as "fun." And what was worse was that she had drawn-out-lazy-vowel-syndrome too as if she was creating her own accent. But for tonight it was fine. I would just drink more.

"Soooooo this is really your plaaace?"

"Yep."

"It's soooo fuuuun!"

"Thanks. What's your name?"

"Susaaaan."

"Where are you from, Susan?"

"Clevelaaaand."

"Ah, the mistake by the lake."

"Heeey! Be niiiice." She gave me a playful punch that I caught in my hand as if I were fielding a baseball.

This was a good sign. It meant that she was interested. Perhaps I was in. Maybe I could even convince her to expand her repertoire of adjectives over morning coffee at Oslo if we got that far. Before I could utter another word, however, suddenly standing in the doorway, through the crowd of people, there she was—none other than Maya.

Maybe Duncan and she were through. After all, Haggis can give you really bad gas, so maybe she had just had enough. She might as well just give me a chance. After all, Maya and I had Hebrew and a Jewish history in common. Maya, Maya, Maya. Even her name sounded like a song.

"Can we back up a second, Matt? I know you wanna talk about Maya, but before we get too far along in your tale of woe, whatever happened to Xandra!?"

"Oh. Well, she did text me one more time at some insanely late hour although I never answered. Thank you for reminding me."

"Well this is important information Matt! What did she say?"

"It was cryptic. All she texted me was, 'Thank you for understand-ing.'"

"That's what she texted you?"

"Yep."

"What the hell does that mean?"

"Phil, I don't know and I never want to know."

"Excuse me for a second, I'll be right back," I told Susan from Cleveland even though I had no intention of returning.

Maya saw me and waved. She was dressed casually: ripped jeans, boots and a white sweater, making her stand out in the hipster soup of people. She had brought a bottle of wine. I went to her and we hugged.

"Well, well, you made it."

"Yes," she answered in her soft voice.

"Come on." I grabbed her hand and pulled her along toward my room. "Let me show you a great view of the city. It's perfect for your wine."

I was kind of amazed that she was actually sitting there with me in my room. It wasn't like we really knew each other and it had taken the moving of an entire mountain to get her to hang out with me in the first place.

She asked me to play a song on the banjo, but instead I said we should write a melody together. It wound up being a short ten-second chorus that had no words to it. It was just a melody, just "la la la." It had a minor-modal quality to it, perhaps not sad, but definitely serious, like something you would hear in the opening or closing scene of a García Lorca play. We sang it through a couple of times before it fell apart with us laughing at ourselves for how stupid it really sounded.

"I love your voice," I said.

"Shut up. You're just saying that."

"No, really! And your name too. Like the song." Maya was a rock standard by the Israeli singer-songwriter, Shalom Hanoch. The only reason I knew this was because I had bought his mid-aughts unplugged album on CD the year I had lived in Israel. I was expecting this comment to impress her, but instead her face just soured.

"Thanks, that's what my ex used to say."

"Oh, I'm sorry." But I wasn't really. Did this mean that Maya was single? Maybe I had a chance.

"No, it's fine. We've been done for a while now."

The mood in the room had changed. Maya stared off into the distance and was obviously thinking of some memory of him. I could tell that she had no interest at all in hooking up. Her energy had been endearing and intimate, but like the older sister tone I remembered from the night we met in Israel the first time. None of her gestures suggested any type of romantic interest. I had gotten as far as I could with her and that was fine. We had had a nice evening together and now it was time to move on. Perhaps we'd be friends.

"It's just so hard to make sense of though," she said, and I could tell she needed someone to talk to.

He ex was an Israeli novelist and they'd had a two-bedroom apartment in the Brooklyn neighborhood of Carroll Gardens. Things had been going fine. Then one day at the dinner table with her sister's family out on Long Island, he simply announced that he wasn't interested in having children.

"Just like that, he said, 'I don't want kids.' I was just as shocked as everyone else. That was the beginning of the end, even though we tried to make things work for a little while longer."

Maya thought being away from the craziness of New York would rejuvenate things for them so they went to Israel together. One weekend when she was visiting her parents in her hometown of Netivot, she got a phone call from a friend that her boyfriend was spotted with another woman in a cafe in Jaffa. She went back to Tel Aviv to end the relationship.

"I remember the last thing that he said as I walked away: 'Maya, don't leave me, I'll kill myself!' Men can be so dramatic. And that's it. That's how it ended, a year ago more or less."

Once she had finished her story, I could tell she was ready to leave. She had gotten it all out and there wasn't much left to say.

"Thanks for having me. It was nice to finally get together after all these years."

We hugged goodbye. I expected her to release the embrace first, but she didn't and we kept our arms around each other for longer than was normal for just friends. I dropped my arms to the small of her back. And then I leaned in and kissed her. I expected her to pull away, but she kissed me back. I went along with it like it was no big deal but in my head, I was excited like Rocky at the top steps of the Philadelphia Museum of Art with my arms raised, screaming, "Adrian!"

I got a blanket from my room and led her up to the roof, the buildings of Lower Manhattan twinkling in the skyline.

"*Nu, bo Nizdayen k'var,*" she whispered into my ear. I realized she was using the word "penis" as a verb and in the reflexive conjugation: *Nu, bo Nizdayen k'far* (let's *penis* already).

"You wanna penis someone?" I asked. The moment I said this, I not only felt like an idiot, but I could tell by the look in her eyes that she simply wanted to get laid. *Nizdayen* was some type of slang term for fucking. "Mati, *fuck* me. *Achshav*. Now." She obviously cared little for the etymology of the word. Instead she was all business. She was my Israeli army commander in basic training—and now it was time to do pushups and run laps too.

She mounted me without any further discussion and inserted me into her immediately. I was shocked by the immediacy of the warmth I felt that happened so quickly. Earlier that night her gestures were that of "Don't start with me" and now we were fucking (or I was *penising* her, as she would say). She rode rhythmically and majestically. She leaned over and uttered the greatest word ever: "*Ken.*"

"*Who's Ken?*"

"*No, Phil. It means 'yes' in Hebrew. She was liking it.*"

"*Gotcha. It's been a while since I last attended a bar mitzvah.*"

She took my fingers with one hand and began to suck on them, while rubbing herself with the other hand at the very place where we were attached. She bounced up and down making the unmistakable patting sound that echoes when body meets body.

"*Ken*," she continued as the ride changed from a trot to a gallup. "*Kennnn, aya, kennnnn, matoooooki.*" (Yes, oh yes, my sweet.) It was like she was watching her own movie and had forgotten that I was there with her at all. But I didn't mind being an extra in this film. I was amazed that it was all in Hebrew!

"*Ani gomeret!*" She cried into the night, the verb that we used in Hebrew school for finishing our homework, the word that I had eternally attributed to my fifth grade fifty-year-old Hebrew teacher, Morah Zohar. The ten-year-old in me wanted to involuntarily raise his hand and read out loud the Hebrew sentences that my mother had helped me pen the night before while cooking blackened salmon for dinner on a Wednesday night.

"Your homework?" I asked as she was writhing.

"I came."

Ah, so that was what she had finished. It was the first time I experienced a woman having an orgasm in Hebrew.

✧ ✧ ✧

I'd finally found that regular hookup I'd been hoping for. We did it every night the first week we were together. I really just liked sleeping with her so I was happy that she liked it too.

"*Because you were doing it in Hebrew?*"

"*Well, that was definitely part of it, Phil. Come to think of it, Maya was amused that I kept asking her to talk dirty to me in her native tongue.*"

I went to her place every night after work. Around her mattress in her furniture-less bedroom, she had this ritual of lighting three thick round candles and one stick of incense. We listened to her laptop's playlist of Israeli classic rock as we lay there in the nude and smoked cigarettes after we finished: Arik Einstein, Kaveret, Yehudit Ravitz, Josie Katz and Shmulik Kraus, Yoni Rechter and of course the song "Maya" by Shalom Hanoch. It was music I recognized from my year abroad, old hits played on the radio stations Reshet Gimmel and Galgalatz on the buses I rode between Haifa and Tel Aviv. It felt like we were squatters in an apartment in Jaffa, rather than Brooklyn.

Maya still lived in the apartment she had once shared with her ex (not Duncan, but her real ex), but she wanted to move out. There wasn't much left—just a mattress, some paintings, suitcases, a Moroccan table, and a box of a dozen or so books in Hebrew that he had forgotten to take with him. Maya gave me two that piqued my interest, a biography of David Ben-Gurion and a famous novel titled *The Lover* that I had actually read an English translation of when I lived in Haifa.

Figuring it wouldn't take much of my time to help with the move, I helped her pack up the rest of her things. We rented a U-Haul truck and drove out to her family's house on Long Island where she planned to store her belongings.

"So, where did you two meet?" her sister asked me in Hebrew. It was strange to hear a conversation in Hebrew in such a strikingly American-looking house. We were having coffee in the kitchen with windows that looked onto a suburban wooded backyard.

If anything, it was like I was on a new adventure in someone else's movie. I was amazed that I was able to respond in Hebrew to her sister almost effortlessly. Sure, my accent was American and my syntax clunky, but it was more or less workable as I trudged along. The next day at work, I had trouble concentrating. I loved all the time I was spending with Maya but I was also exhausted from the lack of sleep because we were *shtupping* every night. My penis (the noun version as opposed to the verb she had illuminated for me) needed sleep too—maybe even with an ice pack.

I decided to call and tell Maya that I wasn't going to make it that night.

"But *Matoki*, what will I do without you?" she complained playfully, but I could tell she wasn't happy about it.

"One night. We'll both get a good night's sleep for once."

"I'm not sure what I'll do without you."

"It's not that big a deal. Is it?"

"Matoki, but you're mine!"

"Mine?" I repeated.

"Yes," she laughed. "Mine, mine, mine." It was the first time I heard a different tone in her voice. It was a subtle shift, but still noticeable.

"You're mine." I couldn't get that phrase out of my head for the rest of the day. If anything, she sounded desperate. I didn't like it.

That evening, I was bombarded with texts.

Her: I miss you Matoki.
Me: I'll be back tomorrow night.
Her: You're supposed to say that you miss me too.
Me: Yeah, sure. I do.
Her: Yeah? Sure? It doesn't sound like you care.

Why did it feel like I was all of a sudden being tested? Maybe it wasn't a good idea to sleep with her every night, to help her move her things in the U-Haul, to talk to her sister in Hebrew. Maybe I shouldn't have agreed to take all of her books as well as her Moroccan table that was now in my living room. Had I given her the wrong impression? Did she think she was moving in with me? In the course of one day, I felt as if something had gone awfully wrong and only because I *chas v'chalilah* (God forbid) just wanted to have one night to myself, alone with my penis!

My saving grace was that she was going on tour in two days and I wouldn't have to think about us or Maya's plans for the future. I did agree to see her the night before she left.

"I'm going to miss you when I'm away, *Matoki*." She curled up next to me while she ashed into the tray upon my chest. I lay there in silence, not sure how to respond. "You haven't said that you're going to miss me yet. Not once."

"Sure, I'm going to miss you." I wasn't. But I just needed to get through the night without a scene.

"When did you start saying 'sure' so much?"

"What do you mean?"

"You know what I mean. What's gotten into you?"

We finished our cigarettes and stubbed them out. I got up without saying anything and began to get dressed. I had planned on faking my way through the evening, but I couldn't take it anymore.

"Where are you going?"

"Home," I said.

"Don't you love me?" she suddenly blurted out.

"Love you?"

"Yes. This is what you wanted. You're the one who wanted all of this." She moved her arms in a circular motion in her empty living room. In my mind, I pondered why it wasn't enough that I was sleepless and waddling around with a sore penis. Now I needed to tell this woman standing in front of me who I barely knew that I loved her and was going to miss her? "What do you want?" I asked.

"I want to be with you tonight, on my last night in the city and when I ask you if you're going to miss me, I don't want your response to be, 'yeah, sure.' You've been fucking me, you helped me move my things, you met my family and you can't even say that you're going to miss me? I want you to want this. So say it now."

What was amazing about that moment was that she was absolutely right. We hadn't really discussed anything at all regarding our feelings for each other because our fling had only been going on for two weeks. She was just trying to figure out if this was going anywhere or if she'd be coming home to something when she returned. Why should I have lied? I didn't but it still came out poorly. I just ended things.

"You know what Maya, this is over."

"I knew it! I fucking knew it you fucking asshole, motherfucker." She began to cry while kind of still laughing at the same time at the ridiculousness of the situation. "But you wanted this. This is what you wanted."

We had met on a mountaintop in Israel and then we bumped into each other in a coffee shop two years later. We had made love every night for two weeks. Now it was all coming to a crashing end.

I suddenly remembered that I had her ex's books. "Do you want your books back?"

Apparently, this was not the right thing to say. "Get out and get fucked!" she yelled. "*Ata chara!*" (You're shit).

Of all the things that she had been saying to me in the eternal language that meant so much to me over the course of our time together, that would be the final utterance. I stared at her for a second. And then I just left. I walked to the Carroll Street subway station to take the G train back to Williamsburg.

On the platform I felt sad, but not because Maya and I were now finished. The crazy thing was I did want everything she had just mentioned, but not with her. I missed Johanna, wherever she was. That intense and mysterious attraction for me was still alive. It was just like the lyrics I had written in the song Joey, "Questions ought to make us try a little harder / even if in the end we're meant not to be."

CHAPTER THIRTEEN

Maya and I had only spent two weeks together, but I still felt a nagging sense of guilt for the way we'd broken up. Even though it was a short-lived fling, it felt as if I had done something wrong. I couldn't get those final words she said to me out of my head. The soundbite played over and over again like a skipping vinyl record: "Atah chara (You're shit). Atah chara (You're shit). Atah chara (You're shit)."

I still worried what karmic consequences would come my way because of the abrupt and messy way that things had ended.

"The warts came back, didn't they?"

"No, Phil."

"Herpes then?"

"No."

"Montezuma's revenge?"

"Creative, but still no. I threw my back out."

"Can we go back to Xandra! for a second? I think it's time you come clean about the fact that Xandra! was a man and you totally entertained the idea and you just don't remember because you blacked out."

"Fuck you, Phil. That is not what happened!"

"Oh come on, Matt. You're telling me that this isn't the part of your story that has strange sexual, 'gotcha' blackmail. Especially with that cryptic text from her (or him). It couldn't have ended there!"

"No, Phil! A few weeks after things ended with Maya, all that happened was I threw my back out."

"Brought on by the stress of learning that Xandra! had a cock?"

"Not at all! Unfortunately for you, back pain is the next part of this story and definitely not what you're making up in your head. By the way, Phil, I think you might have died before the culture around this conversation changed. You need to talk about Xandra!'s cock in more respectful terms."

"Should I call it her 'penis' instead?"

"Their penis, Phil. Their."

It was a few weeks before Thanksgiving when I first noticed the pain in my lower back.

The base of my spine was feeling "stiff" all of a sudden like it never had before. Because I had always been relatively athletic and in good shape, I didn't take it seriously and expected it to go away. But it persisted, even weeks after Maya and I had broken up. My range of motion diminished when I swung my arms from side to side and I could barely rotate my torso. When I went home for Thanksgiving, Mom was worried too and gave me a restorative yoga DVD to take back to Brooklyn with me.

As much as Mom loved her yoga, it scared Dad. "Don't do it,

son. You could hurt yourself."

"Oh, Ronnie, stop being dramatic."

"Your mother does headstands and I'm being dramatic?"

On health matters I almost always listened to Mom because she was the only parent who took the time to eat healthily and exercise (as opposed to Dad who drank and smoked). Perhaps yoga was just what I needed.

My first Sunday morning back in Brooklyn, I sat on the floor in the common area of our loft in front of the TV. The woman on the DVD had long golden hair and a slender body that only could stay that thin from a diet of flaxseed smoothies that probably kept her more regular than Dulcolax tablets.

I closed my eyes and attempted to lean into Warrior II. I led with my lower half with one knee sideways and then extended one arm towards the floor. Once I was sufficiently uncomfortable, I had to thrust my other arm toward the sky to hold this ridiculous position. I breathed into it, looking up at the pipes in the ceiling and concentrating on one spot as the flaxseed-smoothie lady was instructing. Jon burst through the door from his bedroom into the living room with a camera as I was mid-posture in my underwear. Apparently, he had been watching me and was now ready to document it for all to see.

"Dude!" I muttered with my chin tucked to my chest. "I'm trying to concentrate."

"Fuck you! Stop doing your dumb yoga and get dressed already. I'm hungry!" He continued to film me.

"Give me the camera!"

"Cockfuck!"

I jumped up and gave him the finger and in that simple motion

I heard a ripple of two consecutive "ca-clacks" coming from my lower spine, which I ignored, figuring that it was just my body adjusting to the poses I was doing for the first time. I went to my room to change. I took a pair of socks from my dresser. I pulled one up over my ankle like I'd done every day of my life. With the final tug of the argyle, there was a razor-sharp of pain that bolted from the base of my spine through my left buttock and then down my hamstring, through my calf and out my heel, like a bullet.

"Oh, that's not good," I said out loud to myself.

The sensation subsided within seconds. I stood up and everything was fine. But I was still spooked because I had never experienced anything like it before. I told myself that I would get it checked out later.

Jon and I went to Kasia's on Bedford Avenue. As we sat eating our eggs and hipster Polish sausages everything seemed fine. But after we paid the bill, I stood up to leave and the sensation that I had felt back in my apartment returned, only this time it didn't stop. I felt the stabbing of a thousand needles along the expanse of some nerve that probably had a proper Latin name and could be found on a high school classroom anatomy chart. Whatever it was called, I now resented its *existensus dominaticus* as it pulsed inside of me, rippling up and down the left side of my lower body, igniting every synapse like the pinball machine that we'd had in our basement as kids. I sat back down.

"What's wrong?"

"I can't walk."

"Come on dude, really?" My brother was in disbelief. He thought I was joking.

"Let me try again."

Jon's demeanor changed when he realized that I was actually in need of real assistance, because I wasn't able to stand for more than ten seconds. He helped me home with my arm thrown over his shoulder and his hand dragging me from my pants down Metropolitan Avenue. I was a soldier in need of the infirmary after a miraculous return from the front after hobbling through barbed wire, dead horses and smoke from overheated howitzers, now with a piece of shrapnel in my ass (even though all I had done that morning was attempt to do yoga and put on my socks).

In bed that night I called home. When Mom picked up the phone I was a little relieved that I didn't have to tell Dad about throwing my back out because I knew he would get upset.

"Hi hun, are you having your friends over tonight to have your little jam?"

"No, actually."

"Why not?"

"I don't feel well."

"Hold on, your father's just getting out of the bathroom, I'm gonna put you on speaker." I could hear her muttering under her breath to Dad, "It's Matthew."

"Oh the prodigal son comes to roost."

"Hi, Dad."

"How did your gig go today banjo boy?"

"He didn't play. He doesn't feel well Ronnie."

"Why?"

"I'm just under the weather." I didn't want to tell him about the yoga.

"A fever?"

"Nope?"

"Diarrhea?"

"No."

"Constipation?"

"Come on Dad, my back is just bothering me!"

There was silence for a second on the other end of the line. Dad was processing what I had just said.

"It was the goddamn yoga, wasn't it?" Now the anger and frustration were bubbling up because to him, yoga was dangerous and I shouldn't have done it in the first place.

"Matt, how bad is it?" Mom asked, concerned.

"I can't walk."

"Fucking yoga!"

"Calm down Ronnie. Matthew, you need to see a doctor."

"How's he gonna go to the doctor when he can't even make it to the bathroom to take a crap?!"

"Ronnie, please."

"How's he gonna give us grandchildren when he can't *shtup* because he threw his back out trying to do a goddamn headstand?"

"Ronnnnnnie!!!! Matt, you really should see a doctor."

✿ ✿ ✿

Those weeks after I threw my back out were some of the most trying moments of my young adulthood.

Sure, I wasn't battling mental health, cancer, racism, poverty, war, the death of a loved one, nor anything that is really noteworthy in the scope of a man's struggle (the closest I had gotten was genital warts). That being said, the physical pain and the limits of what I could accomplish made me feel a sense of utter panic which drove me into a state of complete hopelessness.

For the first two days of my injury, my brother brought me food in bed when he wasn't in class. He also supplied me with a metallic cane with a plastic handle from CVS that would allow me to hobble into the living area if I needed something. With the rhythmic step-and-click of this device (step-click, step-click, step-click) I was a sight to see. Soon Jon had baptized me "Crutchy" (even though I wasn't actually using a crutch).

I was continually bored because there was nothing I could do in my convalescence. Once I had called everyone I could think of, I skimmed Facebook to see what people were doing. Eventually I got tired of being on my laptop and hobbled out to the couch in the living room to watch television in Spanish but that got old too and I went back to lie in bed. Having exhausted all my potential activities as a newly inducted decrepit, there was really only one thing to do.

"Whack off?"

"Ding ding ding Phil!"

Thoughts of masturbation didn't occur to me right away. After all, I was in a lot of pain and preoccupied with the fact that I couldn't even walk. But eventually, after lying alone, hour after hour, my mind turned to *the deed of all deeds*, tempting me, making me think in the softest voice, "Sure, why not now? It's the perfect time, isn't Matt?"

"No, it's not!" I almost heard myself respond alone in bed, "How exactly am I supposed to whack off without being able to make it to the bathroom quickly to dispose of my used tissues?" That was a red line for me. I always flushed.

"Oh, you'll figure it out," replied my sex drive.

It didn't take long for me to just give in to the urge—seconds actually.

On my floor were the socks that I had put on just a few mornings beforehand, the very pair I'd worn out to breakfast with Jon. So this is what it had come to? I was just fine emptying myself into the discarded argyle innocently lying on the concrete floor not aware that it was about to be violated?

I ravaged the first of them like a Norseman in a medieval Scottish fishing village.

"Thank god that's over," I said, promising myself that I would never do such a thing again. But later that night in my boredom when the urge returned for a second round, I thanked God a second time, this time with gratitude that socks have always come in pairs.

Besides masturbating, checking Facebook, eating, going to the bathroom and watching TV in Spanish, I basically lay around hopelessly waiting until my body felt good enough to allow me to walk again. Finally, by the middle of the week I felt like I could at least make it out of the house of my own.

The walk to the subway was a humiliating experience. The stride that I had always taken for granted was replaced with a left hip that seemed simply locked in place. It was as if God was having fun with me and had traded my body for an enfeebled version of myself just for kicks. Even with the aid of my cane, going into the subway felt downright Herculean. I was the guy that everybody passed and huffed and puffed at for creating bottlenecks for the foot traffic on the stairs and escalators.

At the office, it was no better. I felt guilty for having been injured as if I had done something wrong. It seemed like all the teachers eyed me with suspicion, thinking that I had called in sick for fun.

I would have thought the same thing since just the week before, I had been perfectly healthy, running around and popping my head in-and-out of classrooms. Now I exuded an air of fragility when I slithered around the building that for some reason just inspired repugnance.

The only person who didn't seem to judge me was Reggie, the three-hundred-pound security guard from Harlem. He loved to talk nostalgically about the grittiness of his childhood block in a cadence that reminded me of Eddie Murphy's barber character in the movie *Coming to America.*

One day after work as I was walking out the main entrance, I dropped my walkie-talkie by accident. When I reached down innocently to pick it up, forgetting for a crucial second that I was injured, I felt yet again the very "ca-clack" I had experienced the morning I was putting on my sock.

"One of the socks you violated and which now sat in your trashcan?"

"Yes, Phil."

"Very nice, Matt."

Immediately, the shooting pain went up and down my spine just like the first time it happened.

"Oh, that's not good," I said out loud.

"What's not?" Reggie looked around suspiciously, thinking that I was referring to something he needed to take care of. For a second, I could have sworn that he put his hand to his hip as if he was going for a nonexistent gun, even though we were in one of the safest neighborhoods in Manhattan.

"I tweaked something in my lower back this past weekend and I think I just made it worse," I said, holding my hip.

"Oh dammmmnnn," Reggie said, seemingly relieved that the

problem wasn't security related. "You sleep with a pillow between your legs?"

"Um, no?" I said, surprised by his comment.

"Matt, my man," he said, putting his hand on my shoulder, "YOU GOTTA sleep with a pillow between your legs. It's good for your POSture!" he said, accentuating the first syllable of the word.

"Um, okay," I said, wincing from his touch as if I had been struck. Reggie could see the pain on my face. His glance turned to one of real sympathy, the first I had seen all day since returning to work. My back was so bad again from bending over to pick up my walkie-talkie that I had to take a cab home. From the car I called Judith, letting her know that I needed yet another day off. I could tell that she was a little bit frustrated. After all, I had already missed a few days of work and she had been picking up my slack.

"You clearly need medical help." "Okay," I said in monotone and also in denial.

"Matt, I'm serious. You have to see a doctor. Life is hard and out of our control sometimes. Sometimes I'm having a fat day and just need to eat salad, so I know what it's like. Really I do. See a doctor, will you?"

"She really said it like that? Comparing your back pain to feeling bloated?"

"I don't know, Phil. That's how I remember it."

Before going to bed I was able to book a doctor right away in East Williamsburg through some woman working for my insurance company's third party call center. I was at least comforted by the fact that his last name was Levy.

The next morning I was immediately surprised by the doctor's office when I stepped inside. It hadn't been renovated in decades and I was worried that I had found the wrong Dr. Levy. The walls had brown paneling and the place smelled musty. Sitting at a lone metal desk with an ancient clunky computer monitor was a man in his early sixties wearing a jacket and tie, his hair like Clark Gable's. The only thing missing was an ashtray and a cigarette. He smiled and shook my hand with a strong and masculine squeeze.

"Matthew with zee bad back, I presume?" he said with the faintest European accent, though I could not exactly guess which country it was from.

"Yes, Doctor. I'm so relieved to see someone. Can you please help me?"

"Let me zeee what I can dooo!" he said, emphasizing *dooo* as he put his legs together and clapped his heels, the sound reverberating in the small waiting room. It was strange that he didn't look or act Jewish at all. Instead, he was now reminding me less of Clark Gable and more of someone I had seen in a vintage black-and-white picture that was on the tip of my tongue, but was escaping me.

"My poor boy," he said with a pout and a pat on my shoulder. He made an about face, making his way down a corridor that was dimly lit and with flickering lights from asbestos paneling for a ceiling. "Come in here. Shnell, bitter." he said.

"Whacking off, a bad back and now adverbs in German? This chapter is getting really good, Matt, just as I was getting super bored with all of your sex in Hebrew."

Dr. Levy sat on a stool and instructed me to stand in front of him and enact a few basic movements, most of which I could barely do.

"You may have a slipped disk, which you are way too young to have," he said, shaking his head in disbelief. "Once you're better, you'll have to do some physical therapy."

"But how do I get better first?" I asked.

There was a brief pause while Dr. Levy thought of the right course of treatment. In the silence that ensued, it finally clicked who it was he reminded me of. I was transported back to third grade and Morah Zohar's classroom, the same Hebrew teacher who had taught me the word "Gamarti."

It was Holocaust Remembrance Day and she had brought out black and white pictures of all the Nazis who were now burning in "*Azazel*" so that we would never forget their names.

She stood in front of the classroom, flipping through the photos and naming them one by one. "Hitler, Himmler, Goebbels, Eichmann, Göring, Muller." She ended her warning with the most diabolical, frightening Nazi of all, a man who famously injected chemicals into the eyes of Jewish inmates for fun just to see if he could make the colors change. "And this is Dr. Josef Mengele."

"Oh, that's who you remind me of!" I hadn't meant it to say it out loud, but I now had Dr. Levy's full attention.

"Who?" he asked, already looking modest in preparation for the compliment he was sure to come.

I had to think quickly. "Clark Gable! But I'm sure you get that all the time." ,

He shrugged it off and changed the subject. "How about a shot of cortisone?" he said, making me feel like he was honestly asking for my opinion. "Cortisone?" I said, "In my spine? Isn't that a bit extreme?"

He shrugged and pointed toward the examination table.

The rational side of me knew that Josef Mengele was dead. What were the actual chances that he had been cryogenically frozen for a few decades, only to barely evade capture after his thawing, fled

Argentina and subsequently ending up in Brooklyn to practice medicine again for the rest of his days with a Jewish last name? Not too likely. But Dr. Levy looked so much like the picture that Morah Zohar brought out every Holocaust Remembrance Day. Or maybe I had just entered some sort of Kafkaesque vortex brought on by the pain.

"Will it hurt?" I asked.

"Ja, ja, ja, a lot. But you will walk again my boy!"

Minutes later, I was lying on my side with my shirt pulled, feeling the exacting needle penetrating the area of my third and fourth lumber. I writhed in pain for a few seconds as Dr. Levy placed his other hand upon my shoulder.

It hurt like hell. But I was grateful to him giving me back my ability to walk, and not that he was a Nazi about to perform experiments on me.

CHAPTER FOURTEEN

At least I was mobile once more. In theory, anyway. However, I was scared that the slightest unintentional movement would throw my back out again. Other than work, I avoided leaving the house. I even stayed away from the banjo, afraid that playing while standing was too dangerous in my still-fragile state.

The doctor told me that the slipped disc required time to heal, that rest was the best remedy. So on most evenings after work, I'd just go home to eat dinner, stretch, lie in bed with a heating pad, mix red wine with muscle relaxers and fall asleep. I tried to be content that I could walk, albeit slowly, and that I wasn't in excruciating pain. The doctor had also recommended a physical therapist, but that part of his advice I ignored. I knew that my current routine couldn't go on forever, but I just didn't care. I had found a way to feel safe and that was fine with me.

On one of those random weeknights in December, my brother knocked on my bedroom door. "There's a girl here to see you."

"A girl?" For a second I wondered if I had misheard.

"Yeah, she says she's a friend of Ben's?"

Ben was the bandleader for the Firehouse Ramblers. We'd become friends when he came to one of my jams. I had forgotten that Ben and I had spoken and that he was going to send me a "present" while I was on the mend. He hadn't mentioned having someone else drop it off though. That seemed strange.

"And she has cupcakes."

"Cupcakes, huh?" I said, feeling even more confused.

I wasn't in the mood for company. I was content being drugged up, looking awful and smelling awful and pleased when nothing roused me from my solitude. Jon's look, however, made me think otherwise. He was trying to tell me something with his gaze: *She's attractive. Let her into your room.*

A second later, Jon was replaced by a girl in a black pea coat, jeans, boots and a mane of reddish-brown hair who bulldozed into the room with a tray of cupcakes, smiling like she was a contestant on a game show while I was the weird, creepy Alex Trebek in his pajamas.

"Hi!" she said, full of life in a nasally voice. "You look like you live in a scene from *Rent*."

"Hi," I replied, caught off guard by the energy she had brought into the room.

"Here's the cupcakes," she said, placing them on my nightstand as if I was waiting for them.

"Um..."

"And here's the movie," she said, pulling out a DVD from her jacket before I could say anything. "Ben said you'd want this," she said with a wink, "at least according to him, so...whatever. It wasn't my idea."

"What do you mean?"

"You'll see."

"Have we met?" I asked, realizing now that I recognized her.

"Yep. You were talking about a bunch of weird Zionist stuff and getting drunk by yourself."

"At the Parkside Lounge?"

"Yep," she confirmed.

"What was your name again?"

"Jane Pines."

"Right, like the street in..."

"Tel Aviv, at least according to you."

"So you remember."

"Yep. Enjoy the porn with your cupcakes," she said, leaving and closing the door behind her.

I looked at the DVD and realized what movie had been delivered. On the cover were nine faces in tic-tac-toe formation in a take on *The Brady Bunch*, except that every person in every square was a very attractive blond woman. In fact the name of the movie was *Not The Brady's XXX: Marcia, Marcia, Marcia.*

"I know what happens next."

"What's that, Phil?"

"You went to the trash can to reuse your crusty sock, you filthy bastard. I love you, Matt Check!"

When Jane Pines walked out of my room, she was like a vanishing mirage before the eyes of a wandering desert mendicant. The only proof of her was the fascinating and mysterious gifts she had left behind. Jane Pines was a momentary drink of fresh water in a sea of salty emotions churned up by my fear of recurring back pain. The logical next step for me would be to get her number from Ben and reach out to thank her and see if she wanted to get a drink or dinner. That's what the old Matt Check would have done at least. While I wasn't afraid of calling her *per se*, or attempting to get lucky with her either, I knew the potential scenario if such a thing occurred. Sex with Jane would mean me lying there motionless, like a crash test dummy with a cock (which would only work on the off chance that she was into necrophilia).

A week later, I still needed assistance with even the most basic tasks.

"Do you want your dinner in bed?" my brother asked one night. He had just gotten home from his externship shift at Gramercy Tavern.

I didn't answer right away.

"Hello. Earth to Matt Check."

I nodded to communicate that I heard him.

"You okay?" he asked, realizing how loopy I was. "How many valiums did you pop today?"

"I'm fine dude, don't worry. Can you bring another bottle of red wine with dinner?"

He stared at me questioningly. "Yeah, no problem. Wine and a couple of eggs comin' right up!"

I don't know what it was about the way that Jon said the word "eggs," but I just started to cry the moment he left my room. Something in me took stock of the new bottom I had reached in my life. I was single, I was on pills, my cock was chafed and my balls were empty from whacking off too much since there just wasn't anything else to do by myself. My phone buzzed with a text message at that very moment.

"I'm seeing a band at Spike Hill tonight! Want me to stop by when it's over?"

I didn't really process the text because I was so worked up and experiencing a moment of existential panic. That, and the muscle relaxants had kicked in.

My phone buzzed again a few minutes later. I almost yelled at it as I flipped it open, addressing the annoying cell phone itself and not the person on the other end of the line. "What? What the fuck do you want?"

"The show is over. Do you want me to stop by or what?"

It was then I realized that it was Jane. Immediately, I laughed while still sniffling. A sliver of hope for my situation emerged. Was the universe trying to tell me that this new American girl who brought me cupcakes and porn in bed was someone I was supposed to be paying attention to?

That's how I took it at least.

"Sure," I replied. "You'll be here just in time for my brother to bring me wine and eggs in bed."

Within an hour, Jane was in my room, telling me about a new female Grateful Dead cover band she had just seen. There was an energy of excitement and possibility between us. It might as well have been our first date. It was almost as if the meltdown I'd had earlier in the day had never even happened.

I was propped up with pillows in bed like an ailing hipster maharaja, wearing a wife-beater T-shirt and black sweatpants. Jane sat beside me on the divan, like she was nursing me in my final hours. But to me it felt like I was in slacks and rolled up shirtsleeves at a bar in midtown with her, having just ordered us a round of cocktails and with "All Night Long" playing in the background.

"Is it true that you're a Hebrew school principal? You look too young to be in charge of people."

"I mean you're not wrong."

"I had a bat mitzvah," she said, what seemed like a non-sequitur.

"Mazel tov." We both clinked our glasses, "L'chayim."

"But the only thing about it that I remember is that we danced the Macarena at the party."

Something about her comment seemed surprisingly hysterical. I suddenly envisioned a twelve-year-old version of Jane in a mid-nineties dress with shoulder pads and a pearl necklace, doing the hand motions of the Macarena in front of her Bubby and Zayde.

The image made me laugh, but I also found it endearing. Jane seemed so normal compared to the women I had recently been involved with. Compared to Maya's North African sensibility and Johanna's longing for the Palestinian Congo, Jane was a refreshing change. She was from upstate New York, had gone to public school, majored in communications at Ithaca and now worked for her uncle's *schmatta* business in midtown. The idea of her cheating on me with Kofi Annan was something I would never have to entertain.

The night ended with me making a valiant effort to remove myself from the divan and walk her to the door. "Well, good night."

"It was fun. I'd be up for doing it again some time."

"I'd love that," I said.

I moved in to kiss her, which seemed right. I could feel that Jane was just as intrigued by me as I was by her. I was thrown off by a sudden twinge in my lower back. It wasn't the same excruciating pain I'd experienced before, but it was a reminder that I was still injured and unable to handle the most basic movements.

"Ah fuck!" I shouted open-mouthed as my teeth collided with her lips awkwardly. "Sorry," I said in a fearful whisper that could have been mistaken for someone with extreme constipation.

"Oh my god. Are you okay?" Jane put her arm around my waist and did her best to help me to the couch where I fell down quickly and curled into a fetal position. And then in front of this girl who I had just unsuccessfully attempted to kiss, I began to cry. I knew what I must have looked like to her: a soldier in his iced-over foxhole, shell-shocked by repeated enemy bombardments.

"Oh don't cry." She patted me on my arm.

"Just leave!" I said dramatically, "What's the point? I'll never walk again!"

"Oh you're going to be fine."

"This is so embarrassing."

At that point she gave me a final "bro pat" on the arm. "Take care of yourself and give me a buzz when you feel better."

"Okay," I sniffled.

"Let's talk later this week. I'll check in with you to make sure you're okay."

And with that she gave me a final smile, disappearing into the night.

I woke up the next morning with a newfound sense of motivation. I'm not sure if it was totally because of Jane. Maybe I had just had enough of feeling sorry for myself. Whatever the reason, I suddenly met the day with a new vigor. I might as well have suddenly been in a music video with "Eye of the Tiger" as its soundtrack, while I wore a tracksuit and a 1980s Nike striped headband while donning a pornstar mustache.

I dug out the phone number for the chiropractor given to me by Doctor Mengele Levy and I set my sights on getting better. I went three times a week to the physical therapist and even did the dumb exercises I was given to do at home. I began to sleep with a pillow between my knees. Finally, I stopped taking the muscle relaxers and valiums and I drank much more water than wine (the physical therapist told me that this would help too).

One morning in early March, I was on the L train headed into Manhattan when I realized I wasn't in pain anymore.

"Oh my God, I'm on the subway without my cane!" I heard myself say out loud. It was normal for people to talk to themselves so no one paid any attention to me. When I emerged from the subway in midtown, I felt like Frank Sinatra in his sailor uniform singing, "New York, New York, what a wonderful town!"

"We need to celebrate!" I texted Jane from work that day. "Let's get dinner tonight!"

We ate at the noodle bar Momofuku in the East Village. It wasn't like I had gotten out of jail or beat cancer but it felt like Jane and I were celebrating that very thing. We sat in front of bowls of steaming broth, aproned kitchen staff scurrying back and forth, and it felt as if I had turned a corner in my life, that things were going to look up from that point on.

After dinner we stood together just about to part ways underground at Union Square where she would take the 4 or the 5 train towards south Brooklyn and I'd take the L train east to Williamsburg.

"Well, goodnight!" she said.

I hesitated for a second, because what I really wanted was to invite her back to my place.

"Why don't you come back for another drink?" I suggested.

"Are you sure your back can handle me?" she teased. I knew what she was thinking. We had been texting and talking on a regular basis for a few weeks now and yes, she had been on the sidelines of all my physical therapy updates, but did that in fact mean I was really better?

"You're funny!" I said. "Come on, come back with me. Don't you want to?"

"Okay, yes." she said matter of factly.

We made out the whole subway ride home. We were the annoying couple on the train that everyone simultaneously hated and envied.

In my room it didn't take long until all of our clothes were strewn on the floor like some strange avant-garde installation and we were underneath the sheets. We had barely said a word to each other from the moment that she agreed to come over. As I put on a condom, all I got from her was a silent nod and then we both grabbed at each other with fresh intensity. It wasn't long before we were spending all our time with each other: a patchwork of days, nights, and gigs all strung together. Tuesdays were at her place in Cobble Hill where she would cook. Thursdays we'd go out for dinner in Williamsburg. On Friday afternoons, she would meet me at the office and we'd cross the street to the main sanctuary for Kabbalat Shabbat services. Afterwards, we'd walk up to an anachronistic Italian restaurant with zebra wallpaper that I loved, where we ordered pasta and meatballs from waiters with white dinner jackets and bowties, while Frank Sinatra played in the background.

With Jane it felt like I had finally picked the right type of woman. All along I'd needed someone more like me. As if to prove the soundness of my decision, my father gushed over with approval.

"Gail!" my father shouted when I broke the news that I had met a Jewish girl, "Matthew is finally done with the shiksas!"

Click.

"Hi, Matt."

"Hi, Mom."

"Who is she?" Dad interjected.

"Her name is Jane."

"A Jewish girl named Jane? That's kind of odd isn't it?"

"Well she had a bat mitzvah."

"A normal Jewish woman. Finally! Now you won't have to eat Brussels sprouts and fart all the time, like what would have happened with that Brit you found on the subway." But my father wasn't one hundred percent convinced yet. "Did this 'Jane' go to college?"

"Yep."

"Ah, good. And does she have a job?"

"Yes, Dad, she does."

"Even better. What does she do?"

While I decided to leave out the part of the story about the cupcakes and the porn, I did tell him that she worked in the textile industry.

"She's a real keeper, son!" he said.

"Really?" I said, relieved that Ron Check approved. I didn't want to admit that I still needed my father's approval at the age of twenty-seven. Still, a warm blanket of comfort came over me.

That night the sex was even better. When I tried to figure out what made it different, I tried to compare it to Johanna, the benchmark for what I thought making love should be. The difference was this: with Jane, there was no sense of desperation attached to my desire for her.

I felt nothing but triumph as we both finished at the same time. We lay there side by side, still breathing heavily. I took a deep inhale of smoke from a freshly lit cigarette and thought how good it was to be exactly in this place in this moment. "IBS," said Jane.

"What?"

"Do you know what IBS is?"

"Irritable bowel syndrome?"

"Exactly."

I had noticed that Jane used a lot of non-sequiturs but this was a whole new level.

"My sister Annie, she's got it in a really bad way."

"Um...as in..."

"Yes, gas. She's gassy."

We'd just spent the past hour making passionate love. All I wanted to do was feel close to this woman I now thought of as my girlfriend. So I was confused as to why we were talking about her sister's stomach issues.

"She gets it from my mom."

Now she had brought her mother into the conversation?

I shrugged off the sense of unease and soon forgot about it. We went back to our life of late-night bluegrass music in bars. We had interesting conversations over wine and pasta and the sex was back to being great, no weird conversations afterward.

A week later, however, a similar thing happened. I was still breathing heavily from the final moments of passion with Jane when she suddenly brought up her best friend Dara's husband.

"Did I tell you that Steve has a huge cock?"

"What?"

"Steve, Dara's husband. The podiatrist. Huge! Like one of those weird phallic organic squashes! I love being able to tell you things 'poopy.' It's so easy to talk to you."

"*Poopy?*"

"*Yes Phil.*"

"*Jane just throws in a scatological pet name out of nowhere, after talking about her best friend's husband's schlong?*"

"*Yep.*"

"*I like this woman, Matt. She's your Drenka.*"

"*Wow Phil. I'm flattered! Too bad there's no golden shower scene coming.*"

"*Well, with the way you're setting this up, I'd be expecting a Cleveland Steamer.*"

I asked myself if I could live with this weird post-coital phenomenon and an excremental pet name that Jane had come up with for me. I decided I was fine with it. After all, the sex was great. And I actually loved the ordinariness of our routine. Like picnicking in Central Park. Or going antiquing.

One Sunday, Jane found two hand-size cartoon-looking owl bookends in a second-hand shop.

"Aren't these adorable?" She picked them up as if she had found a rare and coveted artifact. It was such an everyday moment, but I felt something I hadn't expected: it was cute that she had found something that made her happy, even if it was an owl *tchotchke*. It made me admit to myself that I was finally in a mature relationship and that it actually felt right.

However, my favorite thing had to be the connection we shared through music. When we weren't at bluegrass jams, I was seated on my sofa with the banjo in my lap, Jane at my side, as I shared with her the songs that chronicled my life. It felt like she was seeing a part of me I couldn't express solely in words.

One night I played her "Drops of Rain" and prefaced it by explaining that I had written the song for the girl I lost my virginity to.

Once the song was finished, she clapped and then laughed. "Got anything more recent than when you were nineteen and playing with yourself?" "Sure," I said and then decided to play her "Joey." When I finished, Jane sat for a second staring off into space. When she finally spoke, the mood in the room had changed. "Who is that for?" she asked, ominously using the present tense.

"Oh, no one." Her sudden change of mood caught me off guard and I wasn't sure what to say.

"I thought you just said that all the songs you write are inspired by things not working out? That was definitely not just for an 'oh, no one' situation."

I was getting more and more uncomfortable and she could see it.

"Looks like I struck a nerve."

"I don't wanna talk about it. Okay?" I heard myself say out loud defensively.

We both looked at each other for a second. This was the first time that things were awkward since the first night we'd met.

Jane was the best thing that had ever happened to me and I didn't want to fuck this up. I needed to make some type of knightly overture and demonstrate that there wasn't even a residual thought of romantic ghosts from my past. I knew how to remedy this situation once and for all: I would unfriend Johanna on Facebook.

One night, when no one else was around, standing at our kitchen island, I typed "Johanna Kahn" into the white search box for the last time.

I pressed "enter," expecting to click "delete" within seconds and be done with it.

What happened instead was an action on my behalf I had not anticipated at all. Johanna had recently uploaded an album of pictures titled "The Princesses of Nolita Winter Gala."

Without skipping a beat, I found myself clicking through every image voraciously, like an 18th-century buccaneer, plundering an undiscovered trove of booty on a Bermuda barrier reef shipwreck. Johanna was wearing a Thor helmet and smiling with a glass of red wine as if she were Queen of the Vikings holding court for a bunch of hipster serfs. Around her were Sofia, the zebra-striped-sweater guy and a thin and perfectly coiffed Manu-like stunt double, standing and reading from a thick book.

There was a faint flutter in my chest. I had to admit to myself that I resented the fact that Johanna Kahn was simply living her life and that I wasn't a part of it. I knew we hadn't worked out. I knew that we really weren't good for each other in the end. So why did it feel at that moment that there was still something unfinished in our business with each other?

I stepped back from my laptop for a second, as if I had accidentally singed my hand on a stove that I didn't know was hot; a burn telling me something about myself and how I really felt. I knew there was more exploration for me to do around a wound I didn't understand, and one I didn't want to understand either. But I was stubborn. Whatever doubt I was feeling and was suddenly faced with, I pushed it down into the depths of me and finished the task I had initially set out to accomplish: I clicked unfriend and slammed shut my Macbook.

For the next few days, there was a certain sense of relief in the decision I had made. Granted, there were a few moments of doubt, given how I had reacted to simply seeing pictures of her. But I also felt good knowing that I had been decisive. I couldn't just keep thinking about Johanna and looking at pictures of her while I was getting serious with Jane.

A week later, I wasn't even thinking about Johanna anymore. So I was completely caught off guard when I received a text from a 347 number.

"Did you really unfriend me on Facebook? WTF?"

It had to be her. I had erased her contact information. I decided to just not answer, hoping it would all go away. *Though it did register that* Johanna had in fact been paying attention. She too had been checking up on me.

A few days later on my way to work as I was scrolling through emails on my BlackBerry, there was a message in my inbox from her. The subject line was "You and me..."

I was expecting a diatribe simply because I didn't want to be friends with her in cyberspace. I considered deleting it, not wanting to feel guilty for attempting to move on with my life. In the end, I decided to read it.

By the first line, I discovered that this was not an angry missive at all. It was nice. In fact, as I got further and further into the letter, I realized that this was the type of communication I had dreamed of receiving from Johanna Kahn.

I know that all this happened for two solid and very valid reasons. The first is that it took me too long to realise that I was madly in love with you and too long to get myself to a place where my heart was free to love you, and too long to trust you enough to imagine building a future with you, one in which you would not join the long list of men who have entered my life, destroyed it a little and left.

I know I hurt you and that I only have myself to blame for the fact that—for now—you do not trust me. You do not trust me not to walk away again, for my love for you to grow boring somehow. I can only give you my word that it wouldn't.

I know for the moment that we both have to move on. I truly hope that we will continue to see each other as friends if you can find it in your heart. For now—take care. I hope to hear from you.

Why now of all times had she chosen to express her feelings for me, to acknowledge that there might still be something there, now that I was in a relationship with someone I trusted? It seemed so unfair, and all of her own doing. I always had wanted to make it work. I had always wanted to be her boyfriend. And now that it was too late, why was she letting me know that she realised-with-an-s that she cared all along as well? And so in my confusion about what to do and what not to do, I had a few beers at a bar on Third Avenue. And by the third beer, I came to the conclusion that one drink with her wouldn't hurt if she wanted to meet up and talk at some point in the future. I told her as much via text, not expecting much in return. So I was surprised when she made herself available just an hour later.

We met at Epistrophy right back where we had started. She greeted me with a ceremonial kiss on each cheek and we ordered two glasses of Montepulciano. She was dressed in one of her signature outfits: dark jeans, a sweater and one of her ascots. If I had been sober, perhaps I would have been nervous. But I'd had several drinks by this point. I wasn't even sure what I was feeling and what was supposed to happen.

"I have something to give you." Johanna took out a small gray photo album and handed it to me. "I made this for us."

I held it in my hands, the word "us" reverberating in the background. I leafed through the pages of pictures that she had printed. It was a testament to our times together. There was one of those candles in a bottle by whose light we made love.

There was a picture of us seated in her apartment just around the corner from Epistrophy on Elizabeth Street, from one of the nights when we talked of art, literature, Africa and Palestine. There was even a picture of her, myself and Manu.

"How is he by the way? He wasn't in any pictures from your Thor hat photo shoot."

"Oh he's far away this month."

"In the Palestinian Congo?"

We both laughed. She got the joke about the way I had come to understand her world. It was a place where she seemed to be doing just fine without me and writing reports for Kofi Annan in cafes that played obscure Velvet Underground outtakes.

She put her hand on mine hand as I leafed through it.

"You wrote me a beautiful email," I heard myself say, looking up at her.

"I meant every word." She squeezed my hand and I squeezed back. "I've missed you," she whispered.

"So have I." I hadn't meant to say it even though I knew it was true.

"So let's try again."

Hearing those words brought out conflicting thoughts, as if there were two different Matts inside of me, both at odds with each other. There was the romantic, the artist and the songwriter that wanted to drop everything, saying, "Go for it. Fuck it. Break things off with Jane and try one more time." There was also the practical and responsible side of me that said, "No! Absolutely not. Don't ruin a good thing. Don't you want to have a relationship and don't you want someone that your parents like too? You can't trust this woman anyway. It didn't work before and it's not gonna work this time."

It was maddening. Johanna Kahn had never been so sincere with me. She was even flirting with just enough something she had never done before—to make her seem accessible, vulnerable and authentic in a way I had never seen before. Could those words, "Let's try again," finally be the real thing?

What came out of my mouth was totally unrehearsed and honestly, it could have been decided by the flip of a coin between these two warring sides within me. "I'm seeing someone else and it's going really well," I admitted in a Henry Kissinger-like monotone. I swirled the wine in my glass and watched the mini-red waves bathe the insides, which was easier than looking her in the eye.

I thought back to the last time I'd seen Johanna naked and felt a twinge of excitement at what it might be like to be with her again, as if I had just taken the first drag of a cigarette in months after promising to quit. This was my desire for Johanna Kahn: there was almost something wrong in it. It was like that moment when God told Abel, "Do not let sin crouch at your door."

"Why can't we just see where things go?"

"Because that never worked before. Why would it work now?"

"You can't be serious?"

"I am, Joey."

"So why are you here? Why did you want to see me?" The tone in her voice had hardened. She was now clearly frustrated that things were not going as planned.

"For closure?" I heard myself ask out loud, not sure what I really wanted to do.

"Closure? You're an asshole!"

"Joey, I…"

"Fuck you," she humphed as she grabbed her purse. She fished out a bill and put it on the bar. She took the album, slammed it shut and pushed it towards me. "Here's your fucking closure." Then she walked out the door.

I looked through the album on the J train back to Williamsburg. When I got outside my building on Hope Street, I threw it away in the alleyway dumpster but not until I saved one picture that she took of me smiling in a purple sweatshirt.

I ended up telling Jane nothing about the unfriending episode with Johanna Kahn. Instead, I asked her if she wanted to move in together.

CHAPTER FIFTEEN

"So, how long have you been together?" The realtor asked innocently as she handed me the pen at our lease signing.

"Oh, just over three months." I was about to scribble my signature on the document making it official. I looked up and saw the realtor's mildly concerned face and suddenly wondered if I was making a mistake.

"Have most of your clients been together longer?"

"Oh, I get all kinds."

"But on average? What would you say is a typical time to be together before moving in?"

"Please. There are no rules when it comes to love." I couldn't make out exactly what she was thinking. But suddenly there was a new pep to her gestures and a huge smile on her face. "Sign right here on this line, please."

I hadn't considered that combining my life with someone else's after three months was "faster than some." Jane and I never talked about it. I asked her if she wanted to move in together, she agreed and that was supposed to be the end of the story. We had found a gorgeous first floor three-room apartment in a renovated brownstone on Willow Place, a quiet street in Brooklyn Heights.

On moving day, after I brought over all of my stuff from Williamsburg in a taxi, I walked over to Jane's apartment to help with her things and was kind of amazed at how much she owned. In fact it took two trips in the van to move everything. As I sat in between two skinny shaved-head Russian movers in the van, the driver tried to strike up a conversation. "Your girlfriend, she has lots of things," he said with both hands on the steering wheel as if he were imparting some communist nugget of wisdom that he had learned during his childhood in Leningrad.

"The following week a trip to IKEA in Red Hook was necessary because we weren't able to fit all of her clothes in the bedroom closet."

"Oh, women love IKEA, Matt. And there's nothing more kärlek than assembling your own furniture with your älskling. Wasn't it fun?"

"It's not my idea of fun, Phil."

"Did you get the Swedish meatballs in the cafeteria?"

"No."

We bought three white plastic closets, followed the instructions and put them all together. At the bottom of each closet was a shoe rack. Jane lined them with her boots, shoes and sandals side by side, like a general asking platoon cadets to fall into formation.

I noticed that in every boot was a bunch of rolled-up old *New Yorker* magazines. If Harold Ross were to come back from the grave, he would have been impressed by the incredible number of copies that lived in our apartment.

I asked innocently why she did such a thing.

"It's good for the leather. It keeps them shapely," she said, as if I was the only one who hadn't gotten the memo.

Two weeks after the move, our apartment began to resemble a home. The middle room was a classic dining chamber with a chandelier and vintage crown molding. The front living room had a fireplace and floor-to-ceiling windows with wooden shutters that looked out onto a quiet and pretty street that could be mistaken for the early 1900s. And we bought two Persian rugs from a Dutch carpet dealer on the Upper East Side that tied the dining and living rooms together.

Just when I was satisfied that we had finally gotten rid of all the boxes and brought some order to our living situation, Jane had a tiny request. "Could we store Annie's bike for a while?" Her sister didn't have room in her studio apartment, so I agreed. We crammed the bike behind the living room couch. I was annoyed, but I told myself that it was worth it to keep Jane happy.

A few weeks later, Jane had another request. "So, Ben called me up and he wants to know if he can store all of his instruments here, while he's figuring out a longer-term solution." What was I going to say, "no?" I couldn't turn down a bluegrass buddy.

The moment he entered the apartment with two mandolins, I actually thought that it would be kind of cool to have two extra instruments lying around.

"Oh, those aren't the only ones," he said.

"There's more?"

"Yep, come help me! Got a bunch more in the back trunk!"

Ten minutes later I was on a ladder shoving instruments into the crawl space in our bedroom.

"I really appreciate this, Matt!" Ben said as he fed me a Martin D-18 guitar. This was followed by two mandolins—the first was Gibson and second was a Loar. Next were a couple of fiddles. It was like we were part of a bluegrass assembly line. Sure, it was cool to have such great instruments in our home, but did Ben have to have so many?

"No problem," I said, though I wasn't happy with the arrangement.

Jane was fine with accumulating more and more things but I couldn't stand it. It occurred to me that if some Khmer-Rouge-like regime were looking to ethnically cleanse well-meaning-stream-lined-minimalist practitioners of *feng shui*, Jane Pines would have easily been a party boss while I, in comparison, would have been whisked away to one of the government-run internment camps awaiting liquidation.

I told myself that everything was going to be fine and that I should be grateful for what I had. Finding a partner was a blessing and the woman I was making a life with was great. My girlfriend was wonderful and loving, was someone I could trust and build a home with. Johanna never would have been able to give me any of these things.

We settled into a routine by the summer. School wasn't in session so I was usually done working by 5 p.m. I'd be in Brooklyn an hour later, where Jane would either cook for us or we would go out in the neighborhood for a bite to eat. Without fail, Jane was always home waiting for me, often talking on the phone to her mom up in Rochester (to whom I swear I once heard her say, "No Mom, we only do it in the morning. He's too tired at night.") or Annie over in Carroll Gardens or her best friend Susan who lived with her husband Marc-the-podiatrist in Tribeca or her other best friend Dara who lived with Steve who was not a doctor but apparently had a huge cock.

"It's just because...yeah...exactly. She wants a ring and Teddy won't...right. He doesn't wanna spend the...that's right five years. FIVE."

"I'm hungry. What are we doing for dinner?" I might interject, worrying that she was talking about *her* sex life as well.

"Two more minutes, poopers."

"Poopers?"

"Yes, Phil."

"Are we just gonna gloss over this, like it didn't happen? Would you like me to make some witty remark about that?"

"No, Phil, frankly I think you've said enough for the moment."

"Hey, you're the one who invited me to this party."

I looked forward to whiskey and cigarettes on the front stoop when I got home from work on weeknights. Jane had kept a bottle of Jameson in the freezer in her old place in Cobble Hill from which I took a nip here and there. But once we were settled into our new apartment in Brooklyn Heights, it became normal for me to have a full glass in our living room every night, whether I was practicing the banjo, watching TV or having guests over.

Every once in a while, I would slightly overdo it. I would wake up on the couch after having dozed off, or having passed out, not remembering how the evening had ended. A glass of warm and un-drunk liquor would be on the coffee table with perspiration around its rim. The TV would be on, the banjo or an open book would be next to me, and I had barely read a page or plucked a note. I would go to the medicine cabinet and take three Advil gel tablets. Then I would go to the freezer and pour myself a night cap to take the pills before a final nip from the bottle for bedtime.

Jane and I had our first vocal disagreement one morning that summer. Her parents were coming into town to see the apartment and wanted to stay with us. She told them that they could have our bed while we would sleep on a blow-up mattress in the living room. I thought it was weird that Jane had even offered for them to stay over. I thought it even stranger that her parents also thought it was a good idea. Did it simply not occur to Jane that we would be playing a game of toilet musical chairs?

"*My* folks would stay in a hotel," I said when she told me the news.

"It's just easier if they stay here."

"No, it's not. Can you convince them to get a room at the Marriott? Ron and Gail always stay at the Marriott."

"Matt, they're my parents. They asked to spend the night. Come on, it'll be fun." Jane put her hand on mine and patted it lovingly, the way my mom used to coax me into shopping with her at Macy's when I was kid. I had to draw the line. Jane could fill her shoe racks with *New Yorker*-stuffed boots and house as many instruments and bicycles for people as she wanted. But I WOULD NOT put myself in the position of possibly running into her mom in the middle of the night while we were both on the way to the bathroom. *No, you first, Leslie. I insist. I'll just wait out here.*

"Well, if that's how you're gonna be, then *I will* call the Marriott," she acquiesced but she didn't seem happy about it.

"Thank God." I was surprised by those two words, how they came out of my mouth and the severe manner in which they were uttered. It was the first time I had ever let any frustration show.

"What did you just say?"

"Oh, come on, Jay. I was joking."

"You didn't sound like you were joking."

Her parents got a hotel room but we spent pretty much every hour of the weekend together anyway. We went to the Neue Galerie on the Upper East Side to look at Klimt. I talked to Jane's dad about our mutual love of literature and history while Jane and her mom checked in about Teddy and the ring that he still hadn't bought.

This was what adult life looked like. You exchanged pleasantries with your girlfriend and her parents, you lived in a home bursting with mandolins, and during the week you went to your grownup job. There wasn't much time for the banjo but at least there were Saturdays when you could entertain a bunch of toddlers with classics such as "Dinosaur for Shabbat" and "Chicken Soup for Shabbat."

Even though I hated Tot Shabbat, I liked Miss Julie and playing with her made Saturdays bearable. We actually had real musical chemistry. There was a certain effortlessness in finding harmony and melody the first time we would work on a new song, even if we were playing to a room full of babies.

One Saturday, as we were tuning up our instruments, she introduced another song we'd be playing.

"Bim Bam?" I asked, repeating what she had just said. "Those aren't even real words."

I could tell she had never actually thought about the lyrics even though she had sung the song countless times before.

"Here, look. There are hand motions too."

"Hand motions?"

"They're very simple. All you do is tell the kids to make fists and then bump one fist on top of the other. Okay?"

Reluctantly, I began the fist bumping, while Miss Julie strummed A minor and began to sing two words over and over again—bim and bam. After two full verses, I counted that both words bim and bam were sung a total of twenty-four unnecessary times.

"Everyone loves the next part."

"There's more?"

"Yeah. All you do is sing 'Shabbat Shalom' and 'hey' over and over again, while raising your hands up in the air. The kids will scream it at the end during the last 'hey' so watch out because it's loud."

Before I could protest, I heard the elevator bell, meaning that the first of the Tot Shabbaters had arrived. It was little Asher, waddling into the room towards Miss Julie with open arms. His parents followed in pursuit, pushing a stroller filled with colorful toys, while toting a diaper knapsack, a lunchbox full of treats and their son's jacket. They moved slowly with and hunched-over shoulders, making it seem like they were losing the energy to keep up with him. They were red-eyed and exhausted. I could already imagine them getting home and telling the relatives who asked about Asher's whereabouts: "We tried. We really did. But he outran us. He was just too fast for us."

"Miss Julie!! Ahh!!" Asher could barely contain his enthusiasm.

It was as if little Asher was cloned shortly thereafter. A dozen more screaming babies and their exhausted parents filed into the room and formed a circle, ready for the service to begin.

"So, Matt, why don't we start with a little Bim Bam," Miss Julie suggested. "What do you say, kids?"

Little Asher in the front of the room had his hand down his black and white checkered shorts, probably scratching his butt, but the minute he heard the magic words, he quickly yanked his hand out to make one of two fists.

"Matt, shall we play it? Whaddya say?" Miss Julie asked me.

All the kids followed Asher in suit and bumped their fists one on top of the other, like they were doing the YMCA at a nineties bar mitzvah.

Miss Julie and I began to sing the words with everyone. "Bim bam, bim, bim, bim bam. Bim, bim, bim, bim, bim, bam."

When we got to the chorus and sang "Shabbat Shalom," all the kids screamed the word, "hey" just like Miss Julie said they would and the sound was like a tidal wave of high-pitched toddler screeching that could have set off a car alarm. And with each subsequent "Shabbat Shalom," the "hey" got louder and louder.

At the final Shabbat Shalom of the entire song, little Asher screamed at the top of his lungs, like he was a Mohican in the middle of a battle with the English invaders, defending the last member of his family who was still alive. "HEYYYYYYY!"

My thoughts turned to Beethoven in perpetual angst from the humiliation of having to give piano lessons to pay for a rent hike in 19th-century Vienna when all he was trying to do was finish "Für Elise" and the "Moonlight Sonata." That's how I felt, except I wasn't a legendary musician. I was just some guy wanting to play his banjo but I had to sing a song called Bim-fucking-Bam instead.

There was one July morning where I was particularly hungover and looking forward to getting home and sleeping it off in my nice quiet home in Brooklyn Heights. But when I walked into the apartment, it was in total disarray. I hadn't exactly been keeping score but I could swear that with every subsequent week, there was more and more shit in the apartment. The changes were subtle and incremental, but they were still real and significant, like the land grabs by the Israeli military in the Occupied West Bank.

"Good one, Matt."

"Thanks, Phil. I have to criticize Israel at least one time in this book to get some liberal sympathy."

"Agreed, it'll be good for sales. That's if anyone buys this thing and has even gotten to this point in your tale of woe."

There were three opened Amazon boxes on the dining room table with linens strewn about. The mandolins too had been taken down from storage and were all laid out on the Persian rug for some unexplained reason. To top it off, Annie's bike had also been fetched from behind the couch and was parked in the vestibule between the living room and the dining room. Jane was in front of a sewing machine singing along to the radio. "You Make My Dreams Come True" by Hall & Oates was playing, whose irony was not lost on me: This was my dream being shattered.

And then I snapped. "For cryin' out loud, Jane, why do we have all these goddamn instruments collecting dust above our bedroom closet while you're on the phone every night telling your mother about how often we fuck!"

At first she let out what I thought was a chuckle. But then she covered her face and began to cry. I was just as surprised as she was with what I had just said. I went to hug her apologetically, but she pushed me away with both arms like bumping a volleyball.

"You yelled at me."

"I'm sorry."

"This has nothing to do with the mandolins. I know what this really is about."

"What do you mean?"

"Matt, I do not want us to fall apart."

"OH, COME ON."

"Why don't you love me?"

As surprised as I was about how I had just acted, I was even more stunned by the veracious clarity that my girlfriend had just unleashed into the world. It was the moment when I needed to say, *I do love you.* Instead I was silent. It was as if she made me see things for what they really were.

"YOU SEE? If you loved me, you wouldn't have talked to me the way you just did. If you loved me, it wouldn't bother you how many instruments there are or how many THINGS I have. You wouldn't obsess over the bodily functions of my parents when they ask to spend the night! Things changed the moment we moved in together. Something is missing between us, Matt. Something shifted in the way you started to look at me, as if you knew all there was to know about me."

"Jane."

"Sure, I'm *great.* Sure, we're *great together.* I've heard you say it time and time again to people. But, I don't want a mechanical relationship. You think you get me? You don't even realize that you see me as plastic, suburban, easy. EASY. I am smart, I am deep, I HURT deeply. I LOVE deeply, I LOVE you, but can't do this alone when someone doesn't LOVE ME and acts like he hates every-single-fucking-thing about me!"

"Well, I don't hate *everything* about you."

"AHHHHHHHHHH!!!" And with nothing else to say, she stormed out of the room.

☆ ☆ ☆

"Things are fine with Jane," I told my brother over beers a few nights later.

He nodded, waiting to hear me out.

"They're fine. Well, except that Jane talks all the fucking time. Talk, talk, talk. It's like she's the windup Energizer bunny. Every night she's on the phone with her mom and when she's not talking to her mom, it's to her sister or friends. And when she talks to me, it's yak, yak, yak. I mean, it's hard to listen to your girlfriend all the time, right? I'd rather just watch Charlie Rose in silence."

Jon looked mildly shocked. I knew I wasn't supposed to talk about my girlfriend this way, but once the words started flowing, I just couldn't get them to stop. "Okay, just one more thing. Jane is chronically early for everything. I can't stand it. The other day we were going to have dinner and she was standing outside the restaurant, waiting for me like I had been late. It's like she has nothing else to do with her time but be with me!"

"Anything else?" he asked timidly.

"Oh the groceries! I can't fucking stand the early-morning hour when the Fresh Direct deliveries arrive. Six in the fucking a.m. bro! I have to get up and help Jane put everything away in the refrigerator. Then we're up and I have to listen to her talk. And she talks about nothing. NOTHING! Like with her mom, her sister, her friends. I just wanna smoke a cigarette. Drink my coffee. Listen to NPR. Take a dump in peace and quiet and not have to listen to her yapping at me while it's coming out my ass!"

Jon didn't seem convinced so I had to deal the final blow. "I think she tells her mother how often we fuck and when! HER MOTHER! I swear I've heard her talk about it!"

Jon looked at me like he had just smelled something really bad.

When I came to the next morning, the first thing I thought of was Jane. I knew from the feeling in my stomach that I wasn't going to be able to retrace the steps back to the side I had come from. I had to do the honorable thing now, which was to end my relationship with her and figure things out for myself.

If we broke up at home and she got upset, I would be forced to sit there alone probably for hours as she processed the information. If we did it in public, it would probably take less time but we'd be sitting on a bench as dusk turned to night with people all around us passing by and knowing what was happening.

It made me think of *Unetanneh Tokef*, the prayer on Rosh Hashanah and Yom Kippur that reflects upon life's fragility and the potential ways that people could die each year to come: who by water and who by fire? Who by land and who by sea? Who at the restaurant and who on the street corner? Who at the grocery store and who at the coffee shop? Who by phone and who by text? Who by email and who by Gchat?

In the end I settled on the sushi place around the corner. That way, if I had to move out that night, at least the awkward walk home together would only be two minutes. It would have people but not be too crowded. It was intimate enough to have a private conversation. And the lighting was dim enough that I wouldn't have to look Jane directly in the eyes. And then there was this: the edamame was salted perfectly.

An hour later she was sitting in front of me, looking happy and refreshed, maybe even a little bit hopeful that I was in good spirits as well. Even though we had been dealing with some conflict there was nothing in her body language or her gaze that made it seem as if she realized that our relationship was about to come to a crashing end while out to dinner. It was either that or she had a great poker face.

"You're not trapped, Matt."

"Right." Maybe I was. Maybe I wasn't. But it was too late now.

"I'm ready to do this," I told her, trying to convince myself.

"Are you sure?"

"Yes hun," I lied. In that moment when I could have done the honorable thing by breaking up with her, I chose the other path. It was easier to stay together even if I was unhappy.

We sat there silently for a few minutes at our table surrounded by other couples having dinner. Eventually, Jane took a deep breath and reached for my hand to squeeze. I could tell that she genuinely cared for me. I cared too. I was just a liar and a coward.

"Don't fuck up a good thing, Matt."

"I won't Jane. I won't."

And so I would make it work. I had no other choice. I could have told the truth but I didn't. It was as if my heart had been biblically hardened like Pharaoh in Egypt who couldn't help but ask for plague after plague from Moses, even though all he really wanted was to let the Israelites go and be left alone to rule and find a brand-new crop of slaves to build his pyramids and constipate them with matzah.

CHAPTER SIXTEEN

The fall of 2009 was not just the time I spent not breaking up and instead making it work with Jane. It was also when I discovered the powers of Korean yoga.

There was a studio just up the block from our apartment on Henry Street, in the heart of Brooklyn Heights. Several times a week I walked past it on my way to work or running errands, until one day I finally decided to check it out.

The waiting area was tranquil. There was a little bonzai plant, the sound of trickling water and the scent of incense. There were six or seven women, all middle-aged. No one was hot, or wearing tight yoga pants. For a moment I thought that I had entered a women's self-defense class because they were all dressed in what looked like Karate gis, just without belts, making them look like white feminine puffy marshmallow creatures with little heads.

A woman approached me, who I quickly assumed to be the instructor since she wore a tan gi making her stand out from the others. She was short and thin and had black hair parted down the center. She also had a wide and welcoming smile.

"*Hwan-yeong.*"

"Come again?"

"*Hwan-yeong.* Welcome! Name?"

"Um, Matt."

"I'm Heejung." She bowed her head with closed eyes and touching palms like she was praying. I felt as if I had just entered a scene from *Tikki Tikki Tembo.*

"Sorry, I think I have the wrong place," I told her.

"Our yoga is called Dahn yoga. It's Korean. You tap your Dahn Jon. It feels great."

Heejung suddenly assumed the position as if riding a horse and began to pound below her navel with the underside of both of her fists in a circular and rhythmic motion. The sound of pat pat pat, made it apparent that she had a strong core. I wanted to laugh out loud because it looked like she was whacking off with both hands.

"*I wish I had known about this when I was alive, Matt.*"

"*I'm sure it existed back then, just not in Brooklyn.*"

"Looks fun." I was already moving towards the door.

"We're starting now. Try it!"

"No, thank you." I turned around. "It's really not for me."

The door was half open as she approached me, putting her right hand on my lower back, right at the spot where I had back issues. "You're stressed."

I turned around in amazement. "How did you know?"

She gave me a silent smile as if telling me she was a mystical guru who knew certain things about myself that she would eventually reveal, but first I would have to take her class. "Tap your Dahn Jon!"

Ten minutes later, after Heejung had lent me a spare gi, I joined the rest of the participants. First we did a few warmup exercises: modified jumping jacks, pushups and lunges. In the background music played with whiny notes, what sounded like the Chinese erhu, which I had only heard in the subway and kung fu movies of my childhood during Sunday marathons on TBS. I imagined at any moment David Carradine would step into the group and pat me on the back. "Good decision, grasshopper. If you cannot be the horse, be the water he drinks from."

"Time for the Dahn Jon!" said Heejung. "Make a circle!"

"Oh, this is getting better and better."

Heejung lowered the lights and turned the music up. The track changed from the soft erhu to something that sounded like Asian techno.

"Close your eyes! Tap the Dahn Jon to the beat. Feel the force of life."

I looked around. Everyone was concentrating, eyes closed, as the sound of the rhythmic pat-pat-pat could be heard along with everyone's breathing.

Following suit, I began to pound the area of my stomach below my navel with one punch after another along to the rhythm of the music. At first it hurt, and I had the stabbing sensation of trying to pee after drinking too much coffee. But about a minute into tapping my Dahn Jon, the whole area around my stomach became warm and a strange calm came over me.

"Wow," I said out loud as I continued to pound.

The more I concentrated on my breathing, the calmer I became. And all of a sudden, it was like I was flying through a sky of Asian techno music in my brand new white gi. I was going up and up, higher and higher. I felt something at the moment that I hadn't experienced in my entire adult life: serenity.

"You're shining," Jane told me when I got home from class.

"I feel amazing."

"I've done yoga and I've never looked the way that you look. What did you do?"

"It's called tapping your Dahn Jon. It's apparently the life force of the body."

A mysterious comfort came over my daily life once I made visits to the yoga studio part of my weekly routine. It was as if tapping my Dahn Jon had allowed me to form a new perspective on my situation. I began to experience gratitude. I was grateful that Jane and I made love regularly. I was grateful for her owls, her sewing machine, her instruments and yes, her stuffed boots too. These things became markers of endearment rather than frustration. I was even able to embrace the conversations she had on the phone with her mother and friends. And any time I felt anxious, I would simply excuse myself for a few minutes, tap my Dahn Jon and everything would be better.

Besides, even Ron and Gail liked Jane. Now I was considering bringing her to their new retirement house in West Palm Beach for the last few days of December. It was our chance for a sunny and relaxing few days away from the craziness of New York.

I called up my parents to tell them the news the week after Thanksgiving.

"How much do you want?"

"I don't need money, Dad. Can't a child call his parents just to say hi?"

"Sure, hi." There was a short pause on the other end of the line. "NOW WHAT?!"

"You know Dad, I *had* some information that would have made you VERY HAPPY, but I'm not gonna tell you now."

"What? What is it, son?" The tenor of his voice suddenly changed. He was as serene and gentle as a Yanni soundtrack.

"A second ago you acted liked you didn't have a son."

"I just remembered that I did. I'll never forget again."

"What's it worth to you?"

"I thought you didn't need money."

"Jesus, Dad! I'm bringing Jane to Florida!"

On the other end of the line I heard what sounded like a loud cough. I knew it wasn't just any cough though. It was the cough of happy disbelief, as if he couldn't believe his luck.

"Is everything okay?" I asked, feigning concern.

"We'll buy the tickets." My father was trying to contain his excitement.

"You DON'T NEED to buy the tickets, Dad! I'm an adult. I can do it myself!"

"What? Doesn't a son need his father anymore?! What am I? Chopped liver? Cut glass? *Un Gatz?*"

"Let him do what he wants, Ronnie," Mom chimed in.

"Oh, come on, Gail. We'll pay for the plane tickets and her parents can pay for the wedding!"

✿ ✿ ✿

I wanted to buy Jane something thoughtful for our one-year anniversary because it seemed like the right thing to do. Too bad I had an awful track record of getting presents for friends and loved ones. We weren't a gift-giving gift-receiving family, not even for birthdays and holidays. Dad instead gave us one-hundred-dollar-bills and then told us that we didn't call him enough. I was suddenly in uncharted territory.

I went to Bloomingdale's on a Friday afternoon in early December. Jane had already left to go visit her parents. Since we would be spending the end of the year in Florida, she would first go to Rochester to celebrate Hanukkah with her family.

As I strolled through the main floor of Bloomie's, the place was filled with festive holiday cheer. Everywhere I looked people were doing their shopping, red-faced New Yorkers wearing winter coats, argyle scarves and furry Holden Caulfield hats.

"Do you see anything you like?" asked the girl standing behind the jewelry counter.

"I'm looking for something for my girlfriend. It's our anniversary."

"Aw, that's so sweet. How serious are you?" she asked innocently.

"What do you mean?"

"The two of you? How's it going?"

For a second I felt as if there was some higher deity testing my resolve and asking me if I really understood how I felt about my relationship. "We're doing pretty good I guess?"

"$1,000 good, $600 good?"

I now understood what she was getting at. "Oh, much lower."

"$400?"

With my right index finger I pointed downwards. How much was my relationship worth? I couldn't put an exact money figure on it, but $400 seemed a bit excessive.

"Okay." The girl swiftly and eagerly laid out a variety of bracelets and necklaces from under the glass case, all of which were between $80 and $200. "Here are a couple of things that might interest you. These are actually very reasonable, especially for an anniversary."

It turned out that even $200 jewelry didn't look all that attractive. There were several gold brooches, rings with teeny red stones that were probably garnets and not rubies, and a collection of silver jewelry that seemed a little less than spectacular. I wasn't sure what Jane would like from the whole buffet.

Then I spotted it. Right between a silver tennis bracelet and a plain gold ring, there it was: a pair of owl earrings.

"How much are those?"

"Really?" the girl asked in surprise.

"Yes."

"Those are $50, sir."

"I'll take 'em!" I said without skipping a beat.

Her whole body language had changed. I could tell that now she thought I was cheap.

"What? My girlfriend loves owls. Really."

"Would you like a gift-wrapping voucher?"

"No, thanks. I always use old newspapers." This was our family custom for wrapping gifts, the few that we bought.

That night my phone buzzed with a text from Jane.

> *Jane:* I'm sad that you are not with me this weekend :-(
> *Me:* Why?
> *Jane:* It would just be fun having you play board games with the family. :-)
> *Me:* Yeah. :)
> *Jane:* Well, good night grundle-ishess. Plotzky on your face!

"You know Matt...between Jane's excremental preoccupation and your Korean masturbation friends in the last few pages, I'm reminded of the reasons I keep hanging out with you."

"If only I were making it up."

And all of a sudden, this wasn't about board games anymore. I saw something sinister in those sad face/happy face emojis. I felt like I was being misled. My father had teased me about Jane's parents paying for a wedding. Now I wondered if Jane's parents were pondering the same thing.

I was overwhelmed with paranoia and fear of a future I didn't seem to have any say in. I was like a hamster on a wheel that was scurrying and scurrying, running for its life from Richard Gere and his ass. I imagined the conversation that had taken place:

"So when is he going to propose?"

"Mom, I doubt he's proposing."

"Why not sweetie? You're living together and he's taking you to Florida. I bet he's got a ring!"

I suddenly found myself responding to this imaginary conversation from my couch in Brooklyn Heights:

A ring Leslie? What do I know about rings? I'm barely willing to buy your daughter owl earings for 50-fucking-dollars, let alone attempt to even wrap them in legitimate wrapping paper. I'm nowhere near the thought of buying something that would symbolize me spending the rest of my life with someone. Why are you already expecting to become machatunim? Because Jane tells you how often we fuck, which I swear I heard her talk about to you?

Standing in the middle of my living room, I found myself tapping my Dahn Jon over and over again, breathing heavily, trying to focus on my life force which would hopefully give me some peace of mind. But it didn't work. Instead, with every tap of my navel, a montage of super-8 movies played in my head. There was our wedding day and there was the cake-in-the-face moment. There was our honeymoon drive up to Niagara Falls with streamers out the back of an old Volkswagen with a sign that read, "Just married." And then the movies jumped ahead forty years and I was an old man in my sixties. My back was hunched over and I had a worn out look on my face and I stared over at a gray-haired Jane and realized that the best part of my life was behind me. I wondered why I hadn't married the woman I loved, why I cared so much about what my father thought of me.

I grabbed the whiskey and took a big gulp straight from the bottle, something I had never done before. Then I returned to tapping my Dahn Jon. I had more whiskey. Then more. The bottle was almost empty.

"By the way, it was a gerbil."

"Thanks for the correction, Phil."

I was in bed when I came to. I wasn't in my bed though. I looked around and was at first confused about where I was. The clarity of the previous evening had begun to fade into the ether shortly after getting Jane's text. What followed was like a big blurry montage of images that I wasn't quite sure I had lived through or simply dreamed: A taxi ride. Kissing in a stairwell. Uncorking a bottle of Montepulciano while slow dancing in a dimly lit kitchen to "A Case of You". Running a bath and getting in. Touching birthmarks and freckles. A body on top of me with my hands caressing it all around. I knew who it was but I was in disbelief.

"How are you, Bello?" Her voice was the first crisp and clear sound I heard. It was not a dream. I was in bed with Johanna Kahn.

"Oh fuck." The ceiling was still spinning from all the whiskey. "I need Advil," I said, covering my eyes.

"One sec." Naked, Johanna climbed over me. We were in a proper bedroom with an exposed brick wall, not her shoebox of a room that I remembered lovingly. She came back with three pills and a big glass of water.

"Thank you."

"I really do love you," Johanna said, as if that were the correct response as I drank from the glass. Not only was there a pounding in my head from the hangover, but also an equally present and rhythmic pulse coming from my heart caused by the shock of where I was and what had happened.

When we got up and had breakfast together in her living room— yogurt, muesli and berries—a moment of my phone conversation from the night before came back to me.

"Well, hello Bello."

"Where are you?"

"I'm home."

"On a Friday night?"

"Yes."

"Are you married?"

"How drunk are you?"

"Very."

"Then come over. I'm in Brooklyn now on Atlantic Avenue. I'll give you the tour."

"Up to anything fun today?" Johanna asked me now, trying to make small talk. I could tell that she was simply expecting to have a conversation.

Was I supposed to act normal? I was still in shock. "Yes."

"Well, what is it?"

I almost wanted to relax into her presence. In fact, hearing the cadence of her English accent reminded me of why I had come to fall in love with her in the first place. It was as if I had been transported to an alternate universe where things had worked out for the both of us. "I have Tot Shabbat."

"Tot Sh'what?"

"It's Shabbat services for families with toddlers."

"That's so cute. I'm off to visit a couple of kids next week myself." She was referring to her sister, brother-in-law and two nieces who lived in Milan where she would be going for Christmas. "One wants to be a princess so I got her a tiara, and the other wants to be a vet so I got her a doctor's smock." She continued to tell me about the rest of her trip. After Milan, she was taking a train to Paris via Geneva. Then after that she was off to Amsterdam to visit a colleague whose husband was in the Dutch Parliament. The final stop was of course London to visit her mum.

"And what are you doing for the holiday?"

"Jane and I are going to..." Maybe the Advil kicked in as I was mid-sentence or maybe it was the reality that there was something very wrong in what had happened the night before. Not only that but I was now condoning its occurrence by sitting and having breakfast with Johanna like it was no big deal when it was the BIGGEST of deals.

"To where?"

"To West Palm Beach to visit my folks."

"Charming," she said sarcastically. "You could leave your girl-friend and come with me. It would be a lot more fun." Johanna was being snarky but I could tell she was also dead serious.

"No, I can't."

"But Bello, you're not happy."

I felt a type of shame that was new for me, the noisy chaos of mixed emotions smashing against one another, as I thought about the fact that my girlfriend was still probably sleeping soundly up in Rochester while I had *shtupped* not just some random one-night stand (as if that would have been somehow acceptable), but Johanna Kahn.

In retrospect, maybe I should have seized the chance that I had now in front of me, to recover the life with Johanna that I claimed to have wanted so badly. But that wasn't the sentiment I felt. It was as if all those anxieties about my trajectory with Jane Pines had never existed in the first place. It was all replaced by a cold calculation that with a little time, the guilt and shame for my actions would pass. Suddenly getting married to Jane didn't seem like such a bad idea after all.

"Where are you going?"

Without explanation, I was picking up my coat from the couch in the other room. I walked for the door and Johanna followed me.

"I have to go home and get my banjo. I have Tot Shabbat in two hours."

"No, where are you REALLY going?"

"Joey..."

"Bello, it doesn't have to be this way. You can change things if you're not happy. We can be together again."

"It's not as easy as that."

"Yes, it is. You're not betraying anyone by being the person you want to be."

It was a simple line that I wanted to believe and though it touched on something deep that I was going through at that moment, it didn't change my mind.

"Where's the Matt that I know?"

"What do you mean?"

"The one that writes love songs on the banjo for the women he falls in love with."

When I kept walking, she called down to me, gripping the railing in one final plea. "Can I write you an email from the road next week?"

I turned, looked up and answered. "Yes, but don't expect a response."

"Oh fuck you!" Her head disappeared, her voice echoing in the hallway, followed by the slam of her front door.

☆ ☆ ☆

The whole week leading up to our trip to Florida I was expecting Johanna to find a way to contact Jane and tell her everything that had happened. However, there was nothing in Jane's mannerisms, nor body language, nor exchanges with me that made me think that she suspected anything at all had transpired in her absence. In fact when Annie had dropped her off at our place in Brooklyn Heights, we even made love right away. Jane had asked me what I was up to while she was gone and I simply told her that I was playing the banjo and drinking whiskey. It was left at that.

I kept waiting for the acts I had committed to mete out a fair punishment, but they didn't. The only sign I got from the universe was when I was wrapping the little box that had the owl earrings in newspaper. When I turned the paper over, I realized something terrible: I had used an article about Tiger Woods and the breaking news about his infidelity.

Still, Jane and I made it to West Palm Beach unscathed and settled into our time with my parents easily and without any type of problem. In fact, I was scarily amazed at how well she got along with them.

"You can't get duck like this back up north, can you Jane?"

It was our second night in Florida and we'd gone to a Chinese restaurant at the strip mall on PGA Boulevard.

"Not really, Ron."

"Where do you and Matt like to get Chinese food?"

"Lichee Nut on Montague Street."

"Sounds like a whorehouse."

"Dad!"

The fact that we had Phish tickets, the premier jam band of our adolescence, came as a welcome distraction. We drove to the Miami American Airlines Arena in my father's Mercedes convertible, on I-95 South on December 28th for the first show of their perennial New Year's run.

Jane and I were at the bar getting a drink when I heard a familiar voice.

"Matt Check." It was none other than Miss Julie, my Tot Shabbat song-leading partner.

I was caught off guard because it was so out of context. "What are you doing here?"

"My bubby lives down here!"

Jane tapped me on the shoulder, signaling me to introduce her.

"Jane, this is Miss Julie, from Tot Shabbat!"

"Oh wow!" They both gave each other a friendly peck on the cheek.

"Miss Julie, I never knew that you liked Phish."

"Well, you never asked."

☆ ☆ ☆

There was silence on our drive home from Miami. It was the type of post-concert catharsis that was just nice to bathe in after swimming in a sea of people for hours that were dancing and singing. I told Jane about a half hour into our drive back up to West Palm Beach that the setlist was classic and that I couldn't wait to tell Jon about it.

"He used to have so many of those guitar solos memorized when he was younger," I explained.

"Does Miss Julie have those solos memorized too?" Jane responded.

Caught off guard by her sarcasm, my throat dropped to the solar plexus. So Jane knew that something was going on, but she had guessed the wrong woman!

"What do you mean?" I asked, doing my best to act unaffected.

"I mean, it seems like you both get along well."

"Oh yeah? Well, that makes sense. I always thought you both looked alike," I said, not certain what I meant, quietly nervous.

"Oh, is that so? That's good. That means if I'm ever not around, you can have sex with her."

For a second, I thought I should come out with it right then and there. It was on the tip of my tongue. *Jane, something has happened but not with Miss Julie. It doesn't matter who it was with. The point is, I'm not happy and I haven't been for a while. I think we should call it quits now. It's been really great. Really it has. But sometimes things just don't work and people have to move on.*

"I'm kidding, Poops-Magoo. KIDDING. Why do you look pale all of a sudden?"

"Pale?"

"Yes, you've gone white."

My hand was shaking on the steering wheel. Thankfully she didn't notice.

"Perhaps I'm just tired."

"Perhaps it's all her pet names."

She put her hand on mine. "I love you *Plotzky*."

It was obvious that I was in the clear and that she'd never have to know if I didn't want to tell her. It was also clear that Johanna hated me wherever she was and that I would never see her again. What wasn't clear was how I was going to be happy if I didn't feel about Jane the way that I wanted to. I felt more stuck in my situation than I had ever felt stuck in anything, ever before in my life.

"It's time to show Jane the DVD of you playing Tevye!" my

father" said to me when I came out of the bedroom for coffee the next morning.

I rolled my eyes. Dad was referring to the fact that I starred as the lead in *Fiddler on the Roof* when I was a high school junior. In a way it was my destiny. My parents had old VHS cassettes of me singing "Tradition" when I was five years old so it just seemed like it was meant to be when I was cast. Since the whole thing had been caught on tape, my parents showed the part where I sang "If I Were a Rich Man" to every living soul that passed through their home.

"DAD, NO."

"Come on. I've got the DVD in my office. Gail!"

"What?!" Mom yelled from the bedroom.

"Fiddler time!"

"DAD. NO MEANS NO!"

"Come on, son. Go get Jane. It'll be fun."

"Ugh," I muttered in protest. I took the two mugs and walked back to the bedroom to give Jane her coffee in bed where I expected her to still be sleeping, prepared to ask her to come into Dad's office immediately to watch the seventeen-year-old me dancing and singing with a fake beard and a pillow for a belly.

"Jane, Dad wants us to…"

She was fully dressed. The bed was perfectly made. Her shirts and undergarments were already folded. She was moving them from the bed into her suitcase as quickly as possible.

"What are you doing?"

"We're finished."

She took my BlackBerry and flung it at me.

I flinched and dropped a coffee cup onto the carpet. "What the fuck?" I said still holding the other mug in my left hand.

"You're such an asshole." I could tell that for the few minutes I had been out of the room she had been crying.

"Jane, what happened?" She continued to pack her bag and ignore me. "Jane!"

"Your girlfriend."

"What? But you're my girlfriend?"

"One of them, you mean."

I wondered how much she knew. Since we'd been in Florida this whole time, it couldn't be more than a text message. I had left my phone in the bedroom when I had gone to the kitchen to get coffee. Johanna must have texted. She must have sent some silly message and Jane had checked the phone. This was salvageable. This didn't have to end so drastically and abruptly because an ex-girlfriend had decided to text me Happy Hanukkah.

"Jane, what's one little text?" I said guessing that was all it was.

"READ THE EMAIL ASSHOLE! I FUCKING HATE YOU."

So it was an email and not a text. I looked at my BlackBerry and saw that it had coincidentally come through at 7:28 that morning and I hadn't seen it when I got up. Why Jane had decided to look at my emails was not the point any longer. I had been caught. But it wasn't until I read the email that I realized just how caught I was:

I just miss you. Still. More than you can imagine. The other Friday night was a confirmation that the magic is still there, that when we take away the current situation and just go back to me and you, it is still there. The magic of kissing and undressing, showering, talking, laughing and drinking wine. It was so surreal and so perfect. It was strange to realize how much I still love you. As we were kissing I could hear myself repeating again and again in my head "I love you, I love you, I love you," like I was always meant to say it, to you. You said that I was the woman of your life and that we would probably be engaged by now. It made me realise that all these months we have been thinking the same thing.

There it was again: *realise*. She was so not American. The thought of it almost made me laugh.

"I'm canceling your anniversary gift," Jane said, pulling me back into the present.

"What did you get me?" I asked out of tone-deaf curiosity.

"A Hebrew Concordance." Jane was now typing furiously on her laptop, pounding each key probably on Amazon.com about to click cancel. "You never shut up about your Hebrew words."

The intention and sincerity of the gift made me forget for a moment that our relationship had just come to an abrupt end. Instead I was impressed. It sure as hell beat the $50 shitty owl earrings that I had bought her and that were wrapped in the face of Tiger Woods. I was jealous that I was not going to be getting it.

"That's so thoughtful."

"OH, GO SUCK A HEBREW COCK!"

"This is the best part of your whole story, Matt!"

"Thanks, Phil."

CHAPTER SEVENTEEN

Jane and I changed our plane tickets and flew home that night. Though we both collapsed into bed and fell asleep together like nothing had happened, it would be the final night that we slept next to one another. When I woke up the next morning, the first thing I saw was her staring at me. I had never seen anyone look at me that way. Her gaze made her seem like a totally different person than the woman I had shared a home with. It was as if she didn't know me, as if staring long enough might bring back the Matt Check she had once trusted and loved. "It's time to pack, Poopsicle," Jane whispered as if she felt sorry for me.

I imagine that most people who had just caught their partner cheating on them would not stick around as they gathered their things to leave. But not so with Jane Pines. It was as if she needed to make her presence known down to the bitter end. She was in the house the whole day talking on the phone, a previously bad habit now run rampant, a cellular binge episode. She paced back and forth calling everyone: Annie, Susan, Dara, Mom, Bubby, someone named Aunt Ida (who I had never heard of before), and even Teddy's girlfriend who was still waiting for Teddy to pop the question.

I packed my things in a quiet and self-reflective rhythm, along to Jane's nasally pterodactyl voice as if it were a song on repeat: "Yeah. Yeah, it's over…Yeah, we're home from Florida…No, I'm not giving him another chance…Yeah, AN EMAIL. No, I'm not joking. I know, it's totally crazy!"

By early evening, I was ready to go. My banjo, my duffle bag and my suit were piled in the dining room next to Jane's sewing machine and her little owls. She had made plans with her sister that night and was going to be leaving in a few minutes.

"Do you have everything?"

"Yeah."

It dawned on me that these were the last moments we were going to be spending together in the house that we had shared for almost eight months. Yes, I would return to get a few boxes that she was allowing me to keep in the basement, which would warrant a conversation, but that final exchange in the dining room before she left was the true and final ending to things.

"What did you say, Matt?"

"Well, Phil, I began to cry."

Maybe it was because I was scared and had no idea what the immediate future held for me. Maybe it was because I felt bad for the way that things had ended up. Whatever the reason, it was a deep, loud and violent bellow, as I stood there in front of Jane sobbing. There was nothing for her to do but reach out and hug me. And then she began to cry as well. We both stood there holding each other like we had both just lost someone close and dear. And in fact, we had: our relationship, which I had killed.

She went to the bathroom to get a tissue and blow her nose. I could hear it land softly in the plastic bag lining of the trashcan. "Well, Matt, I tried," she said, now much calmer.

"I'll leave the keys on the dining room table."

After that, there wasn't much left to say.

I spent the first few days of the New Year on a friend's couch in Carroll Gardens trolling Craigslist for apartments to sublet. It seemed like I was always on the verge of crying but tears wouldn't come. I knew also that I was free to do what I wanted with my life, but the victory felt pyrrhic. I was constantly revisited by the image of Jane, crying and humiliated by me and my cowardice. In a way I was lucky that there was a task at hand: to find a place to live. Otherwise, I might not have gotten off that couch and would have just continued drinking.

I planned to take the first place I found that was relatively close to Manhattan and was affordable. Dad would help too because I was going to have to be paying double rent until the lease was up at Willow Place in April.

First I went to look at a three-bedroom inhabited by an artist couple in their thirties. It was a sixth-floor walk-up in Park Slope. I liked that it had a claw-foot tub and classic octagonal tiles like an old barbershop. It made me think of the opening scene in

Frannie and Zooey, where Zooey takes a bath and shaves, while chain-smoking the entire time. It didn't work out though. They decided to go with a different applicant.

The second place that I looked at was in Prospect Park. It was a room with a single bed in an attic owned by an obese couple in their fifties. They were eager to have me take the room, but I decided it wasn't for me.

The third place was a fourth-floor one-bedroom walk-up in the South Slope. At $1,600 a month, it was twice as expensive as the other places, but I hoped that by spending more money I could get better quality. As I walked there from the R train at the Prospect Avenue subway station, I told myself that short of bedbugs or living next to a nuclear waste site, I would take the apartment if offered. After all, it was just a sublet. This would give me time to look for something more permanent.

When I arrived, a skinny man in his early forties answered the door. He had an unnatural pot belly (probably from too much beer). He wore an old mesh baseball hat with no logo and round spectacles like he was from the cover of *The Saturday Evening Post*.

"Larry?" I asked.

"Yep! You must be Matt. C'mon in." He held out his hand for a jovial shake.

His wife was sitting on the couch in the living room. "I'm Ruth." She waved a baby spoon like it was a wand, feeding a toddler in a highchair, unfazed by the person who had just walked into their apartment.

The place was a discordant combination of different decorating styles. The living room had an old brown and musty carpet. There was a couch, a coffee table, an old TV with wooden paneling with two African figurines on top, standing adjacent to a DVD of Fellini's *La Dolce Vita* (of all movies). There was French folk music playing in the background, a male voice with just a guitar, a genre I wasn't familiar with. There were also multiple beautiful watercolor paintings on the walls, all with different beach scenes. Lastly, the kitchen had old brown fake wooden cabinets that creaked when I opened and closed them and its windows were covered with plastic to keep out the cold for the plants of all different sizes that sat next to the windowsill. There was something both somber and poetic about it.

"You'll have to water the plants every other day. And make sure to talk to them as well. They need encouragement."

"Encouragement?"

"Yes, winters are tough," Larry said in total sincerity as if they were his friends. I looked out the kitchen windows. They looked onto the ramp of the Brooklyn-Queens Expressway where cars whooshed along.

"It's sometimes calming to count them as they pass by."

"Just like the Simon-Garfunkel song about the New Jersey Turnpike and the spy with the microphone in his bowtie."

"What do you know about the CIA?" Larry was suddenly serious. We stood there awkwardly for a second staring at each other.

"Nothing," I said, confused and hoping for him to say something to the effect that he was joking. "It's a song. Don't you know it?"

I decided to pay no mind and chalked it up to misunderstanding. After all, it wasn't like I had many options.

After the short tour, I sat and had a beer with Larry and Ruth (and their baby). I learned that they were from South Philadelphia, where they were moving back for the winter. Amazingly, they were moving in with his parents on the corner of 4th and Fitzgerald

Street, the same corner that my father had grown up on in the 1950s. For a moment, I felt like we were meant to meet and that we were long lost cousins. That was until we began to talk.

"So why are you moving back?" I asked.

"Well, we just can't afford to live here anymore. The CIA is following us anyway."

"What?" I asked. It was the second clandestine comment he had made since meeting him.

"Yeah, you know. They've been listening in on our conversations for a few months now and I just can't take it anymore."

"Larry!" Ruth cut him off, giving him the cue to stop talking.

"Haha. I'm just kidding, Matt," he said, correcting himself. "So you said in your email you're looking to stay for six months?"

"Yes. That would be great."

"That's fine with us. We'll be taking the crib and some things of course. The rest of the furniture is yours. We'll consider extending the lease as well if you like when the time comes."

Even though the CIA comment had made me feel a little uncomfortable, Larry and Ruth seemed perfectly nice and harmless.

The apartment wasn't the greatest place I had ever seen but I tried to look on the bright side: It was a home, it was quiet, it was still in Brooklyn (and close to Jon and Sara who lived in Park Slope Proper) and my commute to work was still not much more than an hour.

In spite of my reservations, Joanna and I did get around to seeing each other again once she returned from Europe. Our first rendezvous turned into one after another until the number of times accumulated quickly. It became normal for us to meet up on Monday and Thursday nights. Instead of Epistrophy in Nolita, we started visiting a bar in Boerum Hill called Building on Bond with low-lighting, exposed pipes in the ceiling, an industrial fan sitting lifeless in the corner, and an old iron dresser that looked like it was probably used to store card catalog slips at a library in the 1940s. When we weren't there, we were at her railroad apartment with exposed brick that looked out onto Atlantic Avenue and just across the street from a mosque.

Soon the people from her life that I had previously met resurfaced like characters in a television series from an earlier season that you never expect to see again. Of course there was her Dutch roommate Sophie who had moved with Johanna. The film-loving-zebra-striped-sweater-guy showed up frequently as well, now yapping about some book he was reading about director François Truffaut. Even Manu made a cameo, coming around for drinks on a cold February night, ranting and raving about his latest stint in the West Bank and the hard time that some Israeli soldier had given him at the Qalandia checkpoint. I could tell that the experience brought out the romantic in him. His eyes glazed over after talking about M16s and aggressive military patdowns by teenage female soldiers.

My time with Johanna almost resembled what things had been like in Nolita almost two years earlier, just a Brooklyn version of it, a little more somber and weathered from our experience at failing to be a couple. From the outside, it might have appeared that things could actually work out for us this time around. But the truth is that I was totally scared of letting her back into my life. I didn't trust her, even if she was now making an effort. I still had the feeling that too many bad things had happened between us and that there was no way to recover the romance we once had. Even with this anxiety, it just somehow kind of happened. Perhaps part of me didn't want to give up on the music that she had inspired me to write and the love I thought it represented in some ideal realm. Perhaps I always made important decisions at bars in the nighttime with a couple of drinks and had to deal with the consequences afterward. Perhaps I was lonely. Whatever the reason, and without putting a label on it, we were dating again.

Still, I tried to put my reservations to one side in honor of Johanna's birthday, to show my cheerier side at her celebration. It was also a going-away party of sorts since Johanna would be spending a couple of weeks as a consultant in East Timor.

At the party, as I watched Johanna talk to her friends, I stood silently, like a *flâneur* in a Parisian street scene staring at everyone as I swirled Montepulciano between my fingers, looking for the legs of the red wine in my goblet while listening to the various languages and English with Indo-European accents that I could not place. Johanna had been walking from guest to guest to say *"Bonjour"* and *"Comment allez-vous?"* when she saw me in the corner and sauntered over to me.

"It's so great that you're here, Bello." She gave me a swift kiss on the neck and then was back into the action of the party, playing the role of hipster socialite that she cherished so much. For a second, my anxiety dissipated and I was reminded of how I had fallen in love with her. I tried to imagine us living together. For a second I allowed myself the fantasy that this was the next step for us when she returned from East Timor. Sophie would move out and I would move in. Johanna would continue to solve the world's conflicts (from her computer hopefully) and I'd play the banjo and continue to be a principal. She'd teach me French and I'd teach her Hebrew. We'd plan our first trip to Europe together and take that train from Milan to Paris like she wanted. And before leaving for that inaugural adventure, I'd tell my friends and family that she was back in my life.

"Do you always drink alone?" asked a woman out of nowhere. She had olive skin and beautiful espresso eyes. She also had an accent that I couldn't quite place, but I guessed she was from an Arabic-speaking country.

"*Kayf haluk?*" I said to her.

I could tell I had surprised her. "Where did you learn Arabic?"

"I once lived and worked in Haifa."

"I'm from Bethlehem."

So she was Palestinian.

"I see you've both met each other. Charming." Johanna had appeared out of nowhere and interjected herself into our conversation. "Yasmin, this is Matt. Matt, this is my Arabic teacher."

"Oh, nice to meet you." We shook hands.

"Joey is a great student," Yasmin said, looking at Johanna almost proudly. "She'll do great in Yemen this summer."

It took a second for me to process what Yasmin had just said. At first I didn't want to believe what I had heard. Had she said something about being gone the whole summer and had I just blocked it out? I knew Johanna had been taking Arabic classes but I thought it was just for fun. I suddenly felt betrayed and I knew that it showed. Yasmin and Johanna stared at each other and then at me, like there was an important memo we weren't aligned on.

"Matt also plays the banjo," Johanna said, trying to change the subject.

"Oh, I love the banjo. What kind of music do you play?"

"Jewish kids' music," I said, finishing my wine.

"I've never heard someone say that before."

"And you won't again either. It was nice to meet you, Yasmin. I hope to talk again soon. Inshallah."

"Inshallah." She was caught off guard by the abrupt end to our conversation.

I wasn't sure what I was feeling exactly. All I knew was that I didn't want to talk about it. "I'm not feeling well all of a sudden, Joey. I'm going home."

"Oh, okay." She could tell that something had shifted in me, but she didn't say anything. She knew the reason, but it wasn't the time to talk about it.

I had already made reservations for us to go to a nice restaurant before Johanna's flight to East Timor. Even though the final inter-action at the party had put me in a foul mood, I decided to keep the date. I was hoping to avoid any conversations that would bring up a negotiation about our future together. I didn't know what I wanted with Johanna Kahn any longer. I was just going to go with the flow and see what happened.

We went to Buttermilk Channel in Carroll Gardens. My brother had recently taken me there for the oysters and duck meatloaf. I had kept the spot in the back of my mind for Johanna's birthday since it had the type of ambience that I knew would impress her: a large room with a twelve-bulb-candelabra chandelier, wooden tables, three white walls and a fourth with exposed brick.

Our waiter had long hair tied back in a samurai ponytail and I took him to be the amiable stock waiter you'd find in any American-style bistro in the heart of Brooklyn. But instead of answering a question with yes or no, he responded with the proverbial "Yeah-no" that had been in vogue for the past few years, and I couldn't decipher what he actually meant.

"So these Long Island oysters are the ones you'd recommend then?" I asked, pointing to the selection on the menu.

"Yeah-no. They're killer."

"Um, so they are or they aren't?"

"Yeah-no." I could tell that he thought he was being totally clear with me. I looked at Johanna and she nodded her approval.

"We'll take the Long Island oysters. She'll have a Prosecco and I'll have a Beefeater martini."

"Yeah-no. Wanna take a few more minutes to look at the menu for your main courses?"

"Yes!" I said in what I hoped was an ambiguous tone.

He smiled and looked content, having not picked up on my irritation. Then he scurried off into the kitchen.

"What's wrong, Bello? Why are you so frazzled?"

"Can't the guy answer a question like a normal person?"

"What do you mean?"

"Never mind."

The oysters came and went. So did our first round of drinks, so we ordered a second. The alcohol had loosened me up, and my anxiety for talking subsided. During the main course I asked Johanna innocently if she was excited about her trip—and regretted it immediately.

She gushed with details. She would plunge herself into the dense jungle of Baucau, arriving there through vast rice paddy fields and long stretches of untouched coasts. In addition to researching the violence of the roaming Polynesian ninjas, she also looked forward to interviewing the village chief who wanted to re-institute the traditional bartering system of giving animals to a person who had been wronged instead of money, the system the government was trying to put in place.

After dinner, I ordered two snifters of Sambuca (with three coffee beans in each glass) and a brownie topped with a lit candle so we could sing and toast to her birthday. But instead of wishing her a happy birthday, something else came out of my mouth.

"To East Timor!" I said.

"To East Timor!" she replied with a raised glass.

"Next it's off to a country where the Mossad had to airlift Jews out clandestinely," I blurted out.

"What is that supposed to mean?" she asked, confused.

"Nothing. I was joking."

"No, really. What exactly are you referring to?"

I realized that she didn't get my reference to the fact that Yemen was an enemy of Israel and that the country had expelled its Jews in the 1950s after Israel became a country.

"*I mean, that's common knowledge Matt.*"

"*Yeah-no, Phil.*"

"Yemen, Joey. It's a dangerous place." But what really bothered me wasn't really that, nor the fact that it was the most ridiculous conversation to begin with. It was the fact that she had made plans for the entire summer without bothering to inform me.

I could tell she was trying to figure out what to say, which made me nervous. She took a deep breath and spilled it out. "Bello, you are someone that I care deeply about. But the truth is, I wanna consider things carefully."

"What does that mean?"

"My therapist says that you're not in a state of mind to freely engage, to open up. I've reflected upon it and want us to continue to enjoy our time together, which is always lovely, but maybe we could be open to new possibilities as well."

"New possibilities?"

"Perhaps we could continue to see each other while seeing other people too. After all, I'm going to be traveling so much anyway. With things open ended, we'd be happier."

"Happier?"

"Yes. I cannot do the drama any longer."

I stared at Johanna for a second in disbelief. It was back to the beginning with her like when we had first met, her need to feel free and casual about things.

"Would you guys like anything else besides the check?" asked the waiter.

"YEAH. NO. SURE."

"So is that a yes or a no, sir?"

"I DON'T KNOW. You tell me! TAKE A STANCE ON SOMETHING, WILL YOU?!"

The waiter was speechless.

We paid the bill and went back to my place. In the morning we drank coffee and watched the cars go by on the highway, making small talk to avoid what we both were thinking. When she left for East Timor, I was left with the fatigue that reminded me of moving chess pieces in a game that had gone on too long and which I wished would finally just end.

✿ ✿ ✿

For the most part, I didn't involve my parents in my personal life. Yes, I ended up telling them about my infidelity (and that's when Dad started calling me Tiger Woods) but I didn't tell them much more than that. But one day my dad picked up on my forlorn tone over the phone.

"Hey, Tiger, women troubles again?!"

"Something like that."

"I don't know how you still have a pecker with all of your girl-friends."

"Ronnie!"

"What, Gail? I'm just saying."

"I don't wanna talk about it," I said to them both.

Then during a silent break in the conversation, something in me shifted and I decided to come clean. I admitted that I had more or less been seeing Johanna since Jane and I had broken up, but that with Johanna things were not going well. And then I began to cry.

"It's going to be okay, son. You were never happy with either of them."

"How did you know?"

"Because I'm your father and know you. Listen, son, we just want you to be happy. That's all that matters."

"Happy?"

"Yeah, happy."

What was the catch? Where was Dad's talk of finding a wife? Where was his dig about me getting married and figuring things out? What about the fact that I had squandered my time with Jane (who loved me) and gotten back together with Johanna who didn't really know what she wanted? What about the fact that I was not figuring anything out at all coupled with the fact that I was more single now than I had ever been?

But there was no castigation and no trial. Instead he was just being loving, lucid and sincere.

"Your father just wants you to be happy," Mom reiterated.

There was a message here. What I needed first and foremost was to be okay on my own. If I could achieve that, the other things would follow.

"Life's too short to be miserable with people you can't stand." My mom, who let my father do most of the talking during our phone conversations, had finally had her say. She was right. It made me wish she'd speak up more often. Then she added, "It's tough enough with the people you can KIND OF stand."

"What's that supposed to mean, Gail?"

"Nothing, Ronnie."

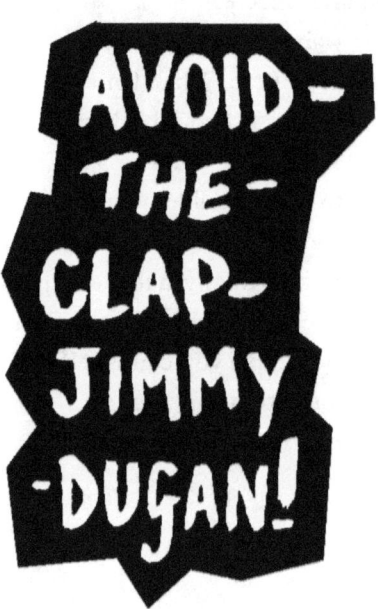

CHAPTER EIGHTEEN

After I spoke to my parents something shifted in me. Apparently the person I *wanted* to be had been ensnared by someone I thought I was *supposed* to be (or rather who I thought my parents thought I was supposed to be). But now I no longer had to live up to an expectation that hadn't even existed in the first place. My father wanted me to be happy, nothing more.

I've always found it poetic that the root of the verb "to release" in Hebrew (*shach'rer*) seemingly shares the same root word as dawn (*shachar*), as if every golden ray of the sun had been held captive by the darkness of night, until it was finally freed, flooding the new landscape of my future. I could now get back to what was important: playing the banjo. Of course, part of me wanted to hold onto the notion that the search for the perfect woman was what drove me to practice the banjo in the first place. Yet as beautiful as this thought was, I finally accepted that my logic had been flawed. Women had let me down and I had let them down too. But my relationship with bluegrass and the banjo was eternal. The goal now was to reclaim this love for its own sake.

I began to gig more. I frequented jams. I said yes to sitting in with various bluegrass bands in the city when asked. I took a gig at The National Underground on Houston and Allen on Tuesday nights. I played at Pioneer Bar-B-Q on Van Brunt Street in Red Hook every other Friday night. I joined a trio at The Double Windsor in Windsor Terrace on Wednesday nights. I returned to the Sunday bluegrass brunch at the Nolita House.

I also started showing up at a jam that everyone talked about: the Saturday night bluegrass jam at Sunny's in Red Hook. It was a hybrid of a hipster destination and a sailor's speakeasy (and an after-hours hangout for the bluegrass musicians once they finished their gigs). The back room looked like an old wooden and creaky dingy. There was an ancient white and faded lifesaver on one of the walls, a painting of a schooner on a second and a lighthouse on the third, up above a wood-colored upright piano that was out of tune.

One night in the middle of a session at Sunny's, a guy with long wavy brown hair and John Lennon spectacles walked into the jam. He ordered a drink and sat in one of the seats observing us stoically. Every time it was my turn to take a solo, I caught him watching me, almost studying my fingers, as I played.

"You're quite a picker," he said when I put my banjo down to go get a drink.

"Phil, are you laughing?"

"No. Okay, yes. But it's not a big deal."

"What is it?"

"You won't find it funny."

"Try me."

"It's just the line, 'You're quite a picker.' It reminds me of my cousin Sylvia when I was growing up. My grandmother would always say to her the exact same words in Yiddish when she caught Sylvia with her finger up her nose, 'du bist gants a piker.' I've never heard the phrase since so it kind of made me laugh."

The guy had a voice that was husky and parched when he told me his name. "I'm Zippo."

"Zippo?" I wondered if he had chosen the nickname consciously or if it had been given to him.

"Yeah. Can I buy you a drink?"

Apart from the strange name, Zippo seemed totally harmless. He was a music producer (or so he claimed), had a studio in the Prospect Lefferts Gardens section of Brooklyn and had recently scored a contract to record the theme song for a new television show.

"Bluegrass on a real television show?" I couldn't think of any other television show to do this other than the *Beverly Hillbillies*, which I remembered from Nick at Nite. It sounded interesting.

"Well, it's not exactly bluegrass."

"So what then?"

"Here."

I watched Zippo shuffle through his iPod. Once he found the song he wanted to play for me, he handed over the earbuds and watched me intently, waiting for my reaction. The first thing I heard was a looped sample of a muddy Dobro playing the same three notes over and over again. And then all of a sudden, a hip-hop percussion track kicked in behind, "Tuk-tuk-chick, a-tuk-tuk-chick. Tuk-tuk-chick, a-tuk-tuk-chick." Listening to it, I suddenly imagined Tupac Shakur on the back porch of an old house in the Mississippi Delta, freestyling with Robert Johnson, the legendary Depression Era guitarist.

"What do you think?" he asked.

He turned to his left and then to his right, looking over both shoulders, making sure no one was watching us or could steal the precious secret that he was on to.

"It's three hours of work for $120 per hour. No credits or roy-alties. You'll have to sign a contract after you record too. Sorry."

Zippo could see the hesitation on my face. I was surprised that there was any money at all, let alone a discussion about royalties.

I thought about this random opportunity that had just come into my life. In my imagination I couldn't have come up with some-thing more distant from my current reality of playing Tot Shabbat songs on the banjo. Furthermore, what business did I have being on a recording that was blending hip-hop and the banjo? And yet I could tell by Zippo's smile that he felt he was about to make music history—and had invited me along for the ride. If anything, I felt flattered and figured I had nothing to lose from the experience. Even if the song turned out to be a disaster, at least I could make a couple of bucks.

"Okay, yes." I reached out and we shook hands.

☆ ☆ ☆

When Zippo sent me the MP3 track to practice for the recording session, I sat on my couch poring over the song with a concentra-tion I had not given the banjo in years. It was reminiscent of the time when I first learned the instrument. And the more I practiced, the more keyed up I became. I started to see the possibilities of this new style of music that he was challenging me to pioneer for the banjo. Maybe I could come up with a hip-hop-hillbilly-dance that they could use in the music video (if there was going to be one).

On the day we were supposed to record, I was expecting Zippo to have a fancy loft since he was a producer, but instead he had a simple place that looked like home to a traditional family. When I knocked I was greeted by a woman I presumed was his wife. She was holding a baby not more than six months old.

"Stu will be right up. He's just setting things up in the basement. Would you like anything?"

"Stu?" I said. So that was his real name.

"Sorry, Zippo," his wife replied, chuckling at his alias. "Would you like something to drink?"

"No, thanks. I'm fine."

I sat down in the family room and waited. The layout, along with the Persian rug and the ceiling's crown molding, reminded me of the house on Willow Place. For a second, I thought about Jane and felt a twinge of sorrow. It was the last thing I expected to be reminded of in that moment.

"I see you found the place." Zippo had come out from behind the hallway banister. He was out of breath from the flight of stairs.

We shook hands and he led me into a cold and dank basement. Tucked in a corner was a whole studio setup: an up-and-running computer with Pro Tools recording software, microphones, headphones, music stands and stools.

"Are you good to go?" He could tell I was surprised by his setup.

I had expected a recording studio, especially for a song that was about to be used on a television show. "It'll do the trick, I promise. Get situated and then we'll get to work."

I put on a pair of headphones and Stu fixed a mic in front of my banjo. The sound of the percussion began: *a-tuk-tuk-chick, a-tuk-tuk-chick.* Then the bass, the Dobro and the scratch guitar track. I started playing the initial rolls and then halfway through during the third measure I hit a sour note.

"Hold on, let me try it again."

"Okay. No problem."

I did a few takes. Zippo and I listened through the tracks together. I could tell by the look on his face that he wasn't satisfied. "It's missing something."

"Like what?"

"Can you try playing less notes?"

I was surprised. The song was already slow as it was. "Fewer notes?"

"Yeah, like this." He patted out the notes on his lap, the way that he envisioned the roll pattern should sound. It seemed like an interesting idea. "It'll make it more syncopated and less busy with that extra space."

"I see what you mean. Let me try."

Zippo pressed record and once the other instruments started, I began to play the roll he requested. Suddenly I locked into the groove and it was like fitting a puzzle piece into its correct place. The look on his face let me know I had nailed it. My rolls lifted up into some sphere on a magic carpet, bringing the song along with it.

After a couple of measures, Zippo made the "cut" sign with his hand. "That's it! You got it. That was exactly what I was looking for."

"Really? It was barely anything. I was just getting started."

"We can loop the rest."

"Um, okay."

I shook hands with him and was on my way. Before I left, he thanked me once more. "You've got exact fingers, Matt. It's really impressive."

Later on I reflected on the day's experience, which was more or less anticlimactic. I was basically asked to play twenty seconds worth of music. And yet, there was a message in Zippo's final comment that continued to marinate in my thoughts. The phrase "You've got exact fingers" made me realize how far I had come in playing the banjo. It made me recall my first banjo teacher so many years earlier teaching me my first rolls when I was challenged to make every note count.

☆ ☆ ☆

What I hadn't ever considered was the possibility that the song would turn out to be an actual success. Not only was it surreal when people heard the sounds of my banjo on television, but now people in the industry were asking when the full-length album was going to come out. But most amazing of all was when Zippo called to let me know that the song had been nominated for an Emmy.

Now I was the source of my father's pride as he bragged about me on the driving range and in the clubhouse.

"He's a Jewish rapper," he told his friends at golf on Sundays.

I wasn't actually, but it didn't matter. My spirits were roused and I felt energized to continue bettering my life. I cut down to three cigarettes a day. I drank wine instead of whiskey. I started going back to yoga and tapped my Dahn Jon regularly before and after work. I even started practicing meatless Mondays.

There was a new bounce to my step when I walked to work in Manhattan after emerging from the subway. At the start of the day I found myself saying good morning to Reggie, Judith and everyone at the office with genuine cheer. And at the end of the school day, I was shaking parents' hands, high-fiving the seventh graders and patting the kindergarteners on the head. It was like I was suddenly wearing all white, snapping my fingers and dancing in a Wham music video.

Every Saturday I would tell Miss Julie about my new musical escapades and one day she suggested celebrating by going out to hear some music. She invited me to meet up with her after work downtown at Googie's Lounge. It was the more intimate upstairs space with tables and couches of another bar called The Living Room.

When I walked in, she waved to me from one of the couches where she had saved me a seat and a glass of red wine. She was wearing skintight jeans and boots with heels. Her shirt was loose fitting and fell off one shoulder. She wore hoop earrings that jangled back and forth. She looked so different, so unlike what she usually wore to Tot Shabbat.

"You look great," I said to her as we clinked glasses for a cheers, almost surprised by what had come out of my mouth.

"Thanks."

The musician at the front of the room placed a harmonica holder around his neck and introduced the song he was about to play.

"Let's see if you guys can figure this one out. I know you'll love it."

He began to strum the opening G sustained chord, which wasn't much of a clue. But with the first pull on his harmonica, it was like a sensor that went off in that part of me that just recognized certain melodies the moment I heard them. They were seared into my subconscious from the innocence of high school days with Jon and Allen when we drove around in our cars, smoking cigarettes and imitating songwriters.

"Are you talking about Nat King Cole?"

"No, Phil. You think I drove around a suburban 1990s high school smoking cigarettes and listening to Nat King Cole?"

It had been so long since I had heard this song in particular, that I could not recall the title though it was on the tip of my tongue. It was about lights flickering in an apartment across the street, about an old rickety radiator and nothing good on a country music radio station. The first verse was like a friend I hadn't seen in years. I was also laughing at the absurdity of the fact that while I had liked it in my youth, I couldn't really have identified with it. How could I have? I was just a nineties suburban kid who had never been to a city. I was in the midst of discovering the banjo and bluegrass and all the music that would come into my life and that I would write: for Paulette, for La Reina de la Stank and eventually for Johanna Kahn.

There was something that was either coincidental or poetic, or maybe even cosmically intended by the universe about what happened next. I was smacked by a karmic chill as the singer arrived at the first chorus, and named the woman the song was about.

"Visions of Johanna." That was the title of the song by Bob Dylan.

I sat with my mouth agape as if there were a spotlight on me, on stage in the closing number of some Broadway classic.

"Everything okay?" Miss Julie whispered, "You look like you've seen a ghost.

"Yeah," I said, shaken from my trance, watching Miss Julie sway back and forth with everyone and enjoying the music.

"I'm great," I said.

The thought entered my mind that perhaps, I had had the wrong perspective all along about Johanna Kahn—and maybe even the idea of love for that matter.

If I had truly loved someone, wouldn't I have loved her regardless of the things that frustrated me? Wouldn't I have been at least a little more patient? That moment was the first time since knowing Johanna that a certain calm descended upon me. I finally felt released from the magical spell of it all, as if this Bob Dylan song were a magic potion.

Those songs that I wrote about Johanna Kahn—it was almost as if I had the foresight to realize that my life would one day be okay. "Even if in the end we're meant not to be."

I watched Miss Julie as she swayed back and forth, laughing and clapping with everyone, enjoying herself.

And suddenly I felt the unmistakable first twinge of attraction. I had always thought that she was pretty, but I had never thought of her in a romantic way. It was something I had never considered before, at least not consciously.

I couldn't help but entertain a flurry of thoughts about us being together. Along with the romance, there'd be an album we recorded together, then a tour, of course.

"And so this is how you finally found the perfect woman?"

"Why would you say that, Phil?"

"Well, Miss Julie seems absolutely perfect for you."

"You've already said that about at least two other women in my book Phil. Do you mean it this time?"

"Yes, I do. And also—I'm trying to speed you up a bit because I'm running out of time and I've gotta get back to that land beyond the River Styx."

"Why?"

"Because the toilets on that side are much better than they are here, you've been going all day and apparently you don't like Nat King Cole."

"I can't believe you're rushing the end of my memoir that I've worked so hard on for so many years, an impassioned tale of love that includes banjo, bluegrass, songwriting, Hebrew, and the evolution of my Jewish identity and meanwhile, you have the chutzpah to leave people with Nat King Cole! I mean, there's nothing wrong with Nat King Cole—he's great. It's just my readers are now being asked to consider the final image of my work in conjunction with one of those compact disc infomercials from the nineties that they used to sandwich between Get Smart *episodes on Nick at Nite."*

"So did you guys shtup or what? Come on. Fess up!"

"No, Phil. Nothing happened."

"I don't believe you. Are you sure you didn't show Miss Julie your 'bim bam' later that night?"

"Phil!" That one was REALLY funny!"

"Well, you said you didn't want to end with Nat King Cole! Nu?"

The fantasy I had conjured up about Miss Julie started out great but soon descended into something dark that was probably much closer to reality.

Everything would be going great with our thriving music careers, our Malibu penthouse, and our Shih Tzu named Oscar until the day that I'd come home to find her sitting on the granite-top kitchen island with José, the Dominican waiter from our favorite Oaxacan restaurant with the ancho chili guacamole that the three of us had eaten together during happy hour, an experience that they were now both desecrating with every smear of Jose's hand across her breasts, an action insulting not only to me but also to all of the Grammys on the wall behind them.

My attraction to Miss Julie was as fleeting as my fantasy and vanished with our goodbyes on the street corner after the show ended. I went home, somewhat surprisingly without her on my mind. Instead I felt a jolt of creativity brought on from hearing "Visions of Johanna" for the first time in many years and the new perspective it had given me.

Alone and by myself at the table in the kitchen with my banjo later that night, I played through a new musical idea over and over again, attempting to work out its shape like a piece of pottery. Chords and a melody emerged over half a pack of cigarettes and a few fingers of whiskey. There was something triumphant and yet somber at the same time in what I was writing. I dashed into the darkness of the living room for a pen and notepad that I had in my suitcase before doubling back to the kitchen table to scribble down my thoughts before they were gone.

"If growin' up means learning how to learn to love again / then I don't wanna be that man / whether blessed or cursed / it's lovely to have met you but it hurts."

I stared at the lyrics for a few seconds. The words were an amalgamation of all my experiences with women up to this point. The names flooded into my mind—Paulette, Isabella, Maya, Jane and Johanna. They were like Xs and Ys in an algebraic equation that all produced the same lonely outcome. Maybe I wouldn't ever find love and I would just keep being a bachelor, living out my days drinking and playing the banjo like someone in a Merle Haggard song. Or maybe, just maybe, I would eventually meet someone with whom I could build a relationship in the way I had seen others around me doing.

It occurred to me at that moment that the Hebrew term for "yore" (*kedem*) is the same root word for "progressing" or "moving forward" (*kadima*), perhaps signifying that the past and the future could be understood as perpetually connected. It was as if the banjo and bluegrass had finally shown me that the only way to forge forward in a better and more truthful manner was to do so while considering the actions of the past.

Before I knew it, not only was the bottle of whiskey finished and all the cigarettes smoked, but the song was done too just as the first light of dawn emerged through the kitchen window.

ACKNOWLEDGMENTS

I am eternally grateful first and foremost to Wendy Dale, without whom this book would never have been written. In 2014, I took an online memoir class with her, and I never imagined it would spark a literary journey (including an actual trip to Bolivia to meet her), which would result in a full-length book about my life. But that's exactly what happened.

Wendy not only helped me find my voice but also gave me the courage to embrace my ideas with conviction. After nearly a decade of editing my work, she likely knows my internal thoughts better than anyone. Without her insight, encouragement and belief in my story, this book would not exist.

I am also deeply grateful to my parents, who have always supported and encouraged me to pursue my passions.

Lastly, I am grateful to my wife and life partner, Lauren. Thank you for being by my side these past few years, listening patiently as I bounced ideas and sentences off of you in the final drafts of the book. Your support has meant everything.

ABOUT THE AUTHOR

Matthew Check is a Cincinnati-based singer/songwriter, multi-instrumentalist and debut memoirist.

A native of Newtown, Pennsylvania, he moved to New York City for graduate studies but soon found himself drawn to the city's thriving bluegrass scene. His career has taken him through unexpected yet deeply formative experiences—from being the first banjo player for Gangstagrass, appearing on their Emmy-nominated track "Long Hard Times to Come" (the theme song for FX's *Justified*), to releasing three albums of Jewish music in the mid-2000s that explored the intersection of tradition and modern folk.

He later stepped into his solo career with *The Condesa Queen* (2020) and *Without a Throne* (2022), blending introspective storytelling with the warmth of 1970s folk-pop.

Matthew lives in downtown Cincinnati with his wife Lauren. He spends his free time walking his dog Oscar Shmulik on the banks of the Ohio River.

ABOUT PARENTHESES PRESS

We Publish True Stories from Unlikely Heroes

These days, the first thing a literary agent asks a writer is not "What is your book about?" or "Do you have a distinctive narrative voice?" but rather "How many followers do you have?"

Parentheses Press is the antidote to this kind of thinking. This small press is the brainchild of author Wendy Dale who grew tired of watching talented writers fail to get published simply because they weren't expert marketers.

At Parentheses Press, we publish great books and then help a writer create their platform. We offer writers multiple ways to connect with readers, including author-led international trips where readers enter a writer's world, quite literally.

We want writers to focus on what they know: writing! And we hope that readers feel the difference it makes when books are selected for their quality, not their marketing potential.

Please sign up to our mailing list below and support great literature. You'll also get information on upcoming trips led by authors.

www.parenthesespress.com/follow-us